EASY LIVIN'
MICROWAVE
COOKING

THE NEW MICROWAVE PRIMER

· ❄ ·

KAREN KANGAS DWYER

· St. Martin's Press   New York ·

Library of Congress Cataloging-in-Publication Data

Dwyer, Karen.
    Easy livin' microwave cooking / Karen Kangas Dwyer.
        p.   cm.
    ISBN 0-312-02910-1
    1. Microwave cookery.   I. Title.
TX832.D98 1989 641.5'882—dc19 89-30119

Second Edition
20 19 18 17 16 15 14 13 12 11

For answers to questions about microwave cooking, send a stamped
self-addressed envelope to Karen Dwyer, P.O. Box 471, Boystown,
Nebr. 68010.

DEDICATION

———— . . . . . ————

I dedicate this book to all new microwave owners, of which I was once one. The amazement at the speed as well as the frustrations of learning to use such a new and totally different appliance are the same for all of us.

This book is my attempt to make microwaving for you what it has become for me—"EASY LIVIN'—like having a household servant!"

I also dedicate this book to my mother, Fern Miller, whose inspiration and patience (especially in cleaning up after all my childhood concoctions) guided me into the home economics field and a love for good cooking.

Last of all, I dedicate this book to my husband, Larry, whose constant encouragement and love for good food brought this book to completion.

CONTENTS

·❄·

EASY
LIVIN'
MICROWAVE
COOKING

—— ····· ——

INTRODUCTION

Your microwave oven is the most exciting kitchen appliance in your home today. It's just perfect for your lifestyle!

- Utility and appliance companies show that you can save up to 75 percent on your energy consumption for cooking by using your microwave regularly instead of your range.

- Your kitchen will stay cooler.

- Your preparation and cooking time will be cut by 50 to 75 percent.

- You will have less cleanup.

- Microwaves are safe for the whole family to use with just a little instruction from you.

- **Best of all it's a fun new world of easy livin' cooking for your whole family to learn and enjoy!**

ANSWERS TO YOUR
MICROWAVE QUESTIONS

———— · ❄ · ————

WHAT ARE MICROWAVES, ANYWAY?

Microwaves are simply electromagnetic waves—similar to radio waves, only shorter. They are nonionizing, unlike X rays, and do not produce any harmful buildup.

Microwaves penetrate food and cause the liquid molecules in food to vibrate approximately 2½ billion times per second. To illustrate how this works, rub your hands together very quickly. You will notice that heat is produced from the friction. This is the same principle under which microwave cooking operates. The water molecules, vibrating at 2½ billion times per second, create friction. This friction produces heat that, in turn, causes the food to actually cook itself.

DO MICROWAVES STAY IN THE FOOD?

Microwaves are only a heating source. Just as no electricity remains in your food when the burner on your conventional range is turned off, so too no microwaves remain when your microwave oven is turned off. However, because the rapidly vibrating liquid molecules in the food do not stop vibrating immediately, the FOOD DOES CONTINUE TO COOK. This is a very important principle of microwave cooking called "standing time."

WHAT IS STANDING TIME?

Standing time is the time that the food continues to cook while the vibrating molecules slow down from the microwaving vibrations of 2½ billion times per second. The microwave oven is shut off. No microwaves are in the food. BUT THE

FOOD IS STILL COOKING! Simply speaking, "standing time" means "let the food stand there and continue to cook without the microwave oven operating."

Standing time is part of the recipe's cooking time. Most recipes will say something like this: Microwave 5 minutes, and let stand 2 minutes. The total cooking time of the food is really 7 minutes.

HOW DOES MY MICROWAVE OVEN WORK?

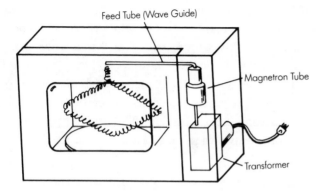

Feed Tube (Wave Guide)

Magnetron Tube

Transformer

The **power cord** conducts electricity to a transformer in every microwave oven. The **transformer** converts low-voltage electricity into high-voltage electricity to empower the magnetron tube. The **magnetron tube** is the very heart of every microwave oven. (It is the primary and most expensive part of any microwave oven and, therefore, the reason why a lengthy warranty from the time of purchase on the magnetron tube is so important to a prospective buyer.)

The magnetron tube produces microwave energy and directs it down a **feed tube** into your microwave oven.

The microwaves bounce off the metal interior of your oven. (All microwave oven interiors are made of metal, but most are covered with acrylic.) Remember these three principles:

1. Microwaves are reflected by metal.
2. Microwaves pass through glass, paper, plastic, and wood products.
3. Microwaves are attracted to water, fat, and sugar.

WHAT UTENSILS OR DISHES SHOULD I USE IN MY MICROWAVE OVEN?

Remember that microwaves pass through paper, plastic, glass, and wood. Therefore, you may:

· Use any paper product: paper cups for hot beverages; paper plates; paper towels; waxed paper; and so on.

· Use any dishwasher-safe plastic containers: plastic bottles; plastic wraps; Styrofoam cups; or boil-in bags. DO NOT USE SOFT PLASTICS, which often melt from hot fat or sugar.

· Use any heatproof glass (Corning Ware; Fire King; ceramics; china; and pottery) that is safe for microwave cooking. DO NOT USE FINE CHINA, LEAD CRYSTAL, OR GLASS TRIMMED WITH METAL.

· Use wooden utensils or straw baskets for short-term heating only. Use toothpicks instead of metal skewers. DO NOT USE WOODEN PLATTERS OR CUTTING BOARDS for long-term cooking. When the water evaporates from the wood, the wooden piece will crack.

Remember that microwaves are reflected by metal. Therefore:

· Do not use metal utensils, except as specified in a convection microwave oven. Many new microwaves allow for the use of small amounts of foil to shield corners of foods, but CHECK YOUR OVEN'S INSTRUCTION MANUAL.

WHEN SHOULD FOODS BE COVERED?

Food should be covered when the recipe recommends it or when moisture or steam should be retained in cooking as in vegetables or casseroles.

- **Cover tightly** means to use a matching lid or plastic wrap. (Leave a small edge turned back on the plastic wrap for a vent so the plastic doesn't split and so a burst of steam does not burn your hand.)

- **Cover loosely** means to use waxed paper, a paper towel, or paper napkin. Moisture and steam must escape from breads and meats to prevent sogginess. Use waxed paper, especially when a sticky food may stick to a paper towel.

- **Microwave uncovered** means the food needs drying rather than moisture and heats quickly. It usually will not spatter.

HOW DO I KNOW WHETHER TO USE THE SHORTEST AMOUNT OF TIME LISTED IN A MICROWAVE RECIPE OR THE LONGEST AMOUNT OF TIME?

Microwave ovens can be purchased in different sizes with varying wattages so a range of cooking times is always listed for each microwave recipe.

- 700-watt ovens cook the fastest. Use the shortest amount of time.

- 650/600-watt ovens cook quickly but not so fast as the 700-watt ovens. Use a time in the middle of the range of cooking times listed.

- 400/500-watt ovens are compact microwave ovens and, therefore, cook more slowly than the mid-size ovens. Use the longest cooking time listed. (Compact ovens often need ⅛ to ¼ more time than a general microwave recipe recommends.)

SHOULD I "ROTATE" OR TURN THE DISH WHEN MICROWAVING?

The ability of microwave ovens to cook evenly has improved greatly during the last five to ten years. Still, some microwave ovens have poor cooking patterns. All parts of the oven often do not receive the same amount of microwaves. The food will be cooked well on one side, and undercooked in the center and overcooked on the other side.

- If you notice the food does not cook evenly in your oven, rotate the dish ¼ turn part way through the cooking time of most recipes (or as directed) to ensure even cooking.

- If your microwave has a turntable, rotating the food may not be necessary.

WHAT SHAPES OF PANS AND FOODS WORK BEST FOR MICROWAVING?

Ring-shaped or round pans work best for microwaving because the microwaves can penetrate the food evenly from all sides.

Ring-shaped pans and foods allow the microwaves to reach the center of foods and, therefore, the center of the food cooks as quickly as the sides and bottom.

Whenever possible, shape foods such as hamburger and meat loaf into a ring or donut shape.

Arrange food in the oven so that the thicker edges are on the outside and the thin and delicate ends of drumsticks, asparagus, etc., are on the inside.

Chicken Drumsticks

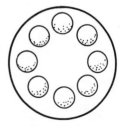

Muffins or Custard cups or Appetizers

WHICH POWER LEVEL SHOULD I USE?

Just as you would not cook all of your foods in a regular or conventional oven at 500°F., so, too, you should not microwave all foods at HIGH (100%).

The various (and lower) power levels cycle the microwave energy on and off to allow for slower and more even cooking. (This allows time for the heat to spread to the cooler and uncooked areas.)

Although many microwave manufacturers have recently tried to standardize the names of the different power levels, many owners still have ovens with varying power-level names. Some microwave ovens even have percentages instead of names for the power levels.

Included in the following chart are the various names used for the different power levels and the percentage of microwave energy associated with each power level.

VARIABLE POWER LEVELS CHART

PERCENT OF POWER	NAME OF POWER LEVEL (DIFFERS ACCORDING TO MICROWAVE MANUFACTURER)	FOODS THAT COOK BEST AT THIS POWER LEVEL
100	High **OR** full power **OR** #10	Small amounts of food that cook quickly plus all vegetables, candies, beverages, and ground meats
70	Medium high **OR** roast **OR** bake **OR** #7	All foods that are to be reheated, plus cakes, bars (cookies), breads, eggs, appetizers, and soups
50	Medium **OR** simmer **OR** braise **OR** #5	Roasts, stews, some cakes, yeast breads, and some quiches
30	Defrost on medium low **OR** #3	All foods that are to be defrosted, plus cheesecakes and tough meats
10	Low **OR** warm **OR** #1	All foods that are to be softened (butter and cream cheese), plus all foods that are to be kept warm

WHAT CAN I DO IF MY MICROWAVE OVEN HAS ONLY ONE POWER LEVEL?

You can reduce the power level HIGH (100%) to MEDIUM HIGH (70%) by placing a custard cup filled with 1 cup of water in the back of your oven. The water will attract some of the microwaves and produce the effect of lowering the power level. This method does not always work perfectly, but many have found it helpful.

Compact ovens (500 watts) may successfully substitute HIGH (100%) power for MEDIUM HIGH (70%) power because the wattages are equivalent.

WHAT ARE "SENSITIVE FOODS"?

Sensitive foods are foods that pop, curdle, or dry out when cooked at HIGH (100%) such as eggs, cheese, mayonnaise, sour cream, mushrooms, or kidney beans. Any food containing these ingredients should be microwaved at MEDIUM HIGH (70%) or lower for any lengthy cooking.

WHAT IS SHIELDING, OR CAN I USE ALUMINUM FOIL IN MY MICROWAVE OVEN?

Shielding means to cover corners of square or rectangular baking dishes or bony pieces and edges of food with foil to prevent overcooking of these areas during microwaving.

- Never cover with foil more than ¼ of the food you are microwaving.

- Never allow the foil to touch the sides of the oven.

- Read the instruction book that comes with your microwave to determine if the manufacturer made the oven to allow for foil. (Check the section of your instruction book under poultry for details.)

For rectangular dishes, cut four 1½- to 2-inch squares or triangles of aluminum foil to cover corners of food and pan, to prevent overcooking and hardening. (For cakes, breads, and bars: remove foil for the last 2 to 3 minutes of microwaving time.)

Wrap aluminum foil around small or bony pieces of meat or poultry to prevent them from overcooking and drying out. (Most meats and poultry pieces need shielding during only half the cooking time.)

HOW CAN I CONVERT MY CONVENTIONAL OVEN RECIPES TO MICROWAVE OVEN RECIPES?

- For best results, follow a similar recipe in a microwave cookbook using your own ingredients.

- Reduce the liquid slightly because very little liquid evaporates during cooking in a microwave oven. Reduce liquid ingredients by one or two tablespoons per cup, as a rule of thumb.

- Read the chapter introduction tips for microwaving in this book for quick ideas to adopt your own recipes for microwaving.

- Plan to reduce the time for conventional cooking by approximately 50 to 75 percent.

- Reduce the amount of your leavening agent (baking powder or soda) by 50 percent.

- Use very little salt on meats and vegetables before microwaving because salt tends to dry out foods during microwaving.

HOW DO I USE A TEMPERATURE PROBE?

The temperature probe is the heat-sensing accessory that comes with many microwave ovens. When it is attached to the microwave oven and programmed, the oven will automatically shut off when the internal temperature of the food reaches the temperature you programmed.

The probe must be inserted two thirds of the way into the center of the food for it to work accurately.

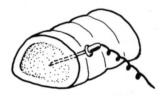

After inserting the probe into the food, program both the temperature and the power level on your microwave oven. (Many recipes have temperatures listed so you can use your probe.) During standing time your food will usually rise 10° to 15°F. more, so temperatures suggested will be lower than those used with a conventional meat thermometer.

The probe will not work for microwaving candy syrups because it programs only to 200°F.

WHAT IS A CONVECTION MICROWAVE?

A convection microwave is fully a convection oven and fully a microwave oven. Simply speaking, convection cooking is "fan-forced hot air." In a convection oven, hot air is circulated throughout the oven cavity by a high-speed fan. The moving air surrounds the food and quickly seals in the juices.

In a convection microwave the microwaves cycle on and off with this fan-forced hot air, producing traditionally browned and crisped foods in half the time of a regular/conventional oven.

Some convection microwave recipes are included in this cookbook, along with adaptations for combining your regular oven with your microwave oven to produce similar results. A variety of convection microwave oven settings are given with each recipe to correspond to the settings on different brands of microwave ovens.

E A S Y   L I V I N'   M I C R O W A V E   F O O D S   C H A R T

FOOD	AMOUNT	PREPARATION AND/OR DISH	MICROWAVE TIME AND POWER
TO DEFROST:			
Meat or hamburger	per pound	wrapped in the package	5–6 minutes at DEFROST (30%)*
Bread slice/bun/ doughnut	per 1	wrapped in paper towel	20–30 seconds at HIGH (100%)
Bread loaf	1 loaf	remove tie, open bag, wrap in paper toweling	1–1½ minutes at HIGH (100%)
Soften hard ice cream	per ½ gallon	in carton	1 minute at DEFROST (30%)
Fruit	10 ounces	pierce bag or place in covered dish	3–5 minutes at HIGH (100%)
Frozen juice	per 6 ounces	remove lid from can	1 minute at HIGH (100%)
Vegetables	DO NOT DEFROST—see COOKING INSTRUCTIONS		
TO REHEAT:			
Dinner plate of food	per 1	food & vegetables on plate	1½–3 minutes at MEDIUM HIGH (70%)
Roll/doughnut/bun	per 1	wrap in paper towel	15 seconds at HIGH (100%)
Sandwich	1 meat, 2 slices bread	wrap in paper towel	1–1½ minutes at MEDIUM HIGH (70%)
Pizza	1–2 slices	place on paper towel	1–1½ minutes at MEDIUM HIGH (70%)
Casserole	1½ quarts	cover	8–10 minutes at MEDIUM HIGH (70%)
Baby food	per 4-ounce jar	remove lid	25–35 seconds at MEDIUM HIGH (70%)
TO COOK:			
Cereal/oatmeal	per ½ cup dry	large bowl, twice as much water	3–4 minutes at HIGH (100%)
Cake	per 1 layer	grease & sugar pan	6 minutes DEFROST & 2–4 minutes HIGH (100%)*
	per bundt	same as above	10 minutes DEFROST & 4–6 minutes HIGH (100%)*
Cookie bars	per 8x8-inch pan	same as above	5–6 minutes at HIGH (100%)
Cupcakes/muffins	per 1	use 2 paper liners	25–30 seconds at HIGH (100%)
	per 6	same as above	2½–3 minutes at HIGH (100%)

FOOD	AMOUNT	PREPARATION AND/OR DISH	MICROWAVE TIME AND POWER
Eggs—scrambled	per 1	dish or Styrofoam cup	40—60 seconds at HIGH (100%)
poached	per 1	2 tablespoons boiling water in custard cup	30—40 seconds at MEDIUM HIGH (70%)
Water/milk/ beverage	per 1 cup	cup without metallic paint	1½—2 minutes at HIGH (100%)
Soften butter	per stick (¼ pound)	on dish	1½ minutes at LOW (10%)
Melt chocolate	per 1 cup chips **OR** per 2 squares	paper plate or dish	1½—2 minutes at MEDIUM HIGH (70%)
TV dinner	per 7 ounce	remove foil lid & place back in box	5—7 minutes at MEDIUM HIGH (70%)
	per 11—20 ounces		8—13 minutes at MEDIUM HIGH (70%)
Meat			
Bacon	per slice	on rack—paper towel cover	30 seconds to 1 minute at HIGH (100%)
Hamburger	per 4-ounce patty	doughnut shape, cover w/paper towel	2½—3 minutes at HIGH (100%)*
Turkey/poultry	per 1-pound whole	on rack	9 minutes per pound MEDIUM HIGH (70%)*
Chicken pieces	per breast (piece)	on paper plate	1 minute HIGH (100%)& 5 minutes MEDIUM HIGH (70%)*
Pork chop	per chop	cover w/waxed paper	1 minute HIGH (100%)& 5 minutes MEDIUM (50%)*
Frozen vegetables	10-ounce box	cook in box	5½—7 minutes at HIGH (100%)*
	16—20-ounce bag	cook in bag or dish	8—12 minutes at HIGH (100%)*
Fresh vegetables	per 1 pound	rinse, cover, no water	7—10 minutes at HIGH (100%)*
Corn on the cob	per 1 ear	in husk or plastic wrap	3 minutes at HIGH (100%)*
Potatoes	per potato (8 ounces)	on a paper towel	4—5 minutes at HIGH (100%)*
Canned vegetables	15-ounce can	covered casserole	3—4 minutes at MEDIUM HIGH (70%)
Soup	10-ounce can	covered casserole w/ 1 can liquid	5—6 minutes at HIGH (100%)

MICROWAVE TERM EQUIVALENTS

HIGH = COOK = FULL POWER

MEDIUM HIGH = ROAST = REHEAT

MEDIUM = SIMMER

LOW = WARM

DO NOT COOK FOODS IN A METAL CONTAINER except for a TV dinner (with foil covering removed).

. . . .

*Add 2 to 5 minutes "standing time" for most foods to complete cooking.

QUICK TIPS AND TRICKS
FOR USING YOUR
MICROWAVE OVEN *

———— · ❄ · ————

Scald milk by microwaving 1 cup milk for 2 to 2½ minutes at HIGH (100%).

Eliminate lumps in white sugar by microwaving it for 10 to 15 seconds at HIGH (100%).

Soften 1 pound brown sugar by topping with an apple slice, covering tightly, and microwaving 1 minute at HIGH (100%) or until softened.

Mix pie crust sticks easily by microwaving each stick for 15 to 30 seconds at HIGH (100%) or until warm, before crumbling.

Dry herbs such as parsley, chives, basil, mint, etc., by placing 1 cup rinsed and paper-towel–dried herbs between 4 paper towels. Microwave for 2½ to 3½ minutes at HIGH (100%). Crumble and store.

Soften cream cheese by microwaving 3 ounces for 30 to 45 seconds at MEDIUM HIGH (70%) **or** 8 ounces for 60 to 90 seconds at MEDIUM HIGH (70%).

Melt chocolate squares or chips by microwaving 2 squares or 1 cup chocolate chips for 1½ to 2 minutes at MEDIUM HIGH (70%).

Melt 1 stick butter (½ cup) by microwaving for 45 to 60 seconds at HIGH (100%).

· ·
*Always use a microwave-safe bowl or utensil when microwaving any food.

Melt 14 ounces caramel candies with 2 tablespoons water by microwaving for 3 to 4 minutes at HIGH (100%), stirring every 30 seconds. This is a great tip for making caramel apples!

Toast coconut by microwaving ½ cup for 1½ minutes at HIGH (100%), stirring twice.

Toast almonds by microwaving ½ cup almonds with 1 teaspoon butter for 1½ to 3 minutes at HIGH (100%) or until crisp and browned, stirring twice.

Resoften gelatin that has set before you remembered to add fruit by microwaving for 1 to 2 minutes at HIGH (100%). Stir, add desired ingredients, and refrigerate.

Proof bread dough by microwaving it in a greased bowl covered with waxed paper for 1 minute at MEDIUM (50%). Let stand 10 minutes and repeat.

Pierce all foods with tight skins or membranes, e.g., egg yolks, potatoes, or squash, to prevent them from exploding.

Stand pierced potatoes on end in muffin cups while microwaving to obtain baked potatoes with drier skins.

Soften underripe avocados by microwaving for 1 minute at HIGH (100%). Cool completely before slicing and mashing.

Squeeze oranges, lemons, and limes more easily and get more juice from them by microwaving one for 30 seconds at HIGH (100%) before squeezing.

Soften hard raisins by microwaving ½ to 1 cup covered with water for 2 to 3 minutes at HIGH (100%).

Defrost a loaf of bread by removing the twist tie (but not the plastic bag) and microwaving for 50 to 75 seconds at HIGH (100%). Let stand 5 minutes to complete defrosting.

Soften hard ice cream by microwaving ½ gallon for 45 to 60 seconds at DEFROST (30%); 1 pint for 15 to 30 seconds; 1 quart for 30 to 45 seconds.

Turn crystallized honey or jam into liquid by microwaving for 20 to 60 seconds at HIGH (100%).

Stack 3 pancakes with 1 teaspoon butter between each, and freeze. Microwave, uncovered, for 1 to 2 minutes at HIGH (100%) to reheat.

Freshen soggy potato chips, pretzels, crackers, or popcorn by microwaving for 45 seconds (per 2 cups) at HIGH (100%). Let stand 1 minute.

Separate cold bacon by microwaving amount needed for 45 to 60 seconds at DEFROST (30%).

Hard-cook eggs for chopping and adding to salads by cracking one egg into a small, lightly greased custard cup. Prick yolk and white with a fork twice and cover with a small piece of waxed paper. Microwave for 1½ to 2 minutes at MEDIUM (50%) or until white is set and yolk is *almost* set. Let stand 1 minute to complete cooking. For 2 eggs: microwave for 2 to 2½ minutes.

Microwave and drain ground beef at the same time by placing it in a microwave-safe colander and setting it in a casserole.

Microwave roasts or whole poultry with very little fat by covering with bacon attached with wooden picks first. The bacon will attract the microwaves evenly and allow browning while basting and flavoring the meat.

Make your own TV dinners by using your leftovers (now called "planned overs") and freezing them in divided paper plates.

Save calories by omitting the butter used in sautéing vegetables, fish, chicken, etc. (Microwaving does not require fat to cook these foods.) Add 1 teaspoon butter after microwaving for flavoring, if desired.

Convert your favorite bar (cookie) recipe to a microwave recipe. Bars that usually bake 25 to 30 minutes will bake in 5 to 7 minutes in your microwave oven. Use a 9-inch pan and shield the corners.

Heat compresses by microwaving a small wet towel for 30 to 60 seconds at HIGH (100%).

Loosen a "stuck" cough syrup or nail polish cap by microwaving for 10 seconds at HIGH (100%). Presto!

Clean and remove cooking odors such as fish or cabbage by microwaving 1 cup water mixed with 1 tablespoon lemon juice or 1 slice lemon for 1½ to 2 minutes at HIGH (100%). The steam will loosen spattered foods and make cleanup easy.

Make dough for crafts by mixing 1½ cups boiling water with 1 cup salt and 3½ cups flour. Knead 8 minutes until firm and add food coloring. Roll dough ¼ inch thick and cut into desired shapes. Microwave four 4-inch objects for 2 minutes at DEFROST (30%) on waxed paper. Let stand 10 minutes and repeat microwaving if needed. Paint and spray with a protective coating or varnish.

Make your own liquid soap for dispensers by mixing 4½ to 5 ounces grated moisturizing soap or leftover soap bits with 3½ cups water. Microwave for 6 to 7 minutes at HIGH (100%), stirring 2 to 3 times. Cool to thicken. Pour into dispensers.

APPETIZERS AND BEVERAGES

———— · · · · · ————

· **Mix dips and spreads in advance.** Heat and spread on canapé crackers and breads just before serving.

· **Choose crackers and breads that are sturdy and crisp** so they don't become soggy when microwaved with spreads on them.

· **Microwave crackers and breads on 2 layers of paper toweling.** The towels absorb the moisture and the crackers stay crisp.

· **Use HIGH (100%) power for microwaving most small appetizers.**

· **Use MEDIUM HIGH (70%) power for microwaving all appetizers and dips** that contain cheese, cream cheese, sour cream, mayonnaise, or mushrooms because these are sensitive ingredients that curdle or dry out.

· **Microwave beverages at HIGH (100%) power** until boiling.

· **Watch milk beverages closely** since they boil over easily when microwaved.

APPETIZERS

· ❄ ·

HOLIDAY CHEESE BALL

———— · · · · · ————

It tastes great; serve it for any occasion.

· CHEESE BALL ·

8-ounce package cream cheese

8 ounces (2 cups) grated cheddar cheese

2 tablespoons finely diced onion

2 ounces (½ cup) crumbled Roquefort cheese (optional)

2 tablespoons blackberry brandy or apple juice

· COATING ·

⅓ cup chopped walnuts or pecans

1 tablespoon dried parsley flakes

1. Microwave cream cheese in a 2-quart bowl for 1 to 1½ minutes at **MEDIUM HIGH** (70%). Beat in remaining cheese ball ingredients with a spoon or electric mixer. Chill slightly and form into a ball.

2. Combine coating ingredients. Roll cheese ball in coating. Serve with assorted crackers.

Yields: 12 to 20 servings.

———— · ❄ · ————

PARTY SNACK MIX

—— · · · · · ——

1⅓ cups thin pretzel
   sticks
1⅓ cups salted mixed nuts
   or peanuts
2 cups corn-squares cereal
   (e.g., Corn Chex)
2 cups wheat-squares
   cereal

2 cups rice-squares cereal
⅓ cup butter or margarine
2 tablespoons Worcester-
   shire sauce or 1 tablespoon soy sauce

1. Combine dry ingredients in a 3-quart casserole. Set aside.

2. Microwave butter and Worcestershire sauce in a small bowl for 1 minute at HIGH (100%). Stir.

3. Pour butter mixture over cereal mix. Toss well. Microwave for 6 to 7 minutes at HIGH (100%) or until cereal is coated and crisp, stirring every 2 minutes. Spread evenly on a paper-towel–lined cookie sheet to cool. Store in a tightly closed plastic bag.

Yields: 9 cups.

—— · ❄ · ——

Variation: You may substitute all nuts for the pretzels or all pretzels for the nuts.

Party Shrimp Dip looks and tastes elegant, yet it can be prepared in just a few minutes. We usually serve this dip in a silver chafing dish, garnished with a fresh sprig of parsley and with a basket or plate of assorted wheat wafers nearby.

Leftover dip may be thinned with milk, heated, and served over cooked rice for a quick entrée.

SHRIMP DIP

———— · · · · · ————

A delicious hot dip for entertaining.

8-ounce package cream
   cheese
10½-ounce can cheddar
   cheese soup

4½-ounce can shrimp
3 tablespoons diced green
   onion

1. Place cream cheese in a 1-quart casserole. Microwave 1 minute at MEDIUM HIGH (70%) to soften.

2. Add remaining ingredients and mix thoroughly. Microwave for 5 to 6 minutes at MEDIUM HIGH (70%) just before serving.

3. Serve warm with assorted crackers. (Dip may also be served in a chafing dish.)

Yields: 8 to 12 servings.

———— · ❈ · ————

Compacts: Microwave at HIGH (100%) instead of MEDIUM HIGH (70%).

SPINACH DIP IN RYE BREAD

. . . . .

1 loaf round crusty rye bread (or bread of your choice)	3 tablespoons milk
	dash of salt
	dash of pepper
20 ounces frozen spinach	dash of nutmeg
2 (8-ounce) packages cream cheese	assorted crackers or vegetables for dipping
1 teaspoon lemon juice	

1. Cut a 1½-inch to 2-inch slice from top of the bread. Cut a circle 1½ inches from outer edge of crust. Remove center, leaving at least 2 inches of bread on bottom. Cut removed bread (center and top pieces) into cubes for dipping and store in a tightly closed plastic bag until serving time.

2. Microwave spinach in packages for 5 to 6 minutes at HIGH (100%) until heated. Drain well. Set aside.

3. Microwave cream cheese in a 2-quart bowl for 40 to 45 seconds at MEDIUM HIGH (70%) until softened.

4. Mix in spinach and remaining ingredients. Spoon into bread. Before serving, place filled bread on a towel-lined plate. Microwave for 50 to 60 seconds at HIGH (100%) until bread is warm. Serve with removed bread and assorted crackers, or vegetables.

Yields: 8 to 12 servings.

———— · ❄ · ————

Variation: For bacon-spinach dip, microwave 6 slices bacon for 4 to 5 minutes at HIGH (100%) until crisp. Crumble. Add ½ cup Parmesan cheese, ¾ cup mayonnaise, 2 tablespoons parsley, ¼ cup sliced green onion, and the bacon to the above recipe. Microwave dip for 3 to 4 minutes at MEDIUM HIGH (70%) before placing in bread.

TIPS
· · · · ·

Warmed Spinach Dip in Rye Bread is always an appealing appetizer in the fall and winter months. Be sure to ask your baker in advance for a round loaf of unsliced rye bread, to make sure it is available when you need it.

TIPS
· · · · ·

Teenagers especially seem to like this delicious and easy party dip. Heated taco chips are the perfect accompaniment. To heat taco chips: microwave 1 to 2 cups of chips on a paper-towel—lined microwave-safe plate for 40 to 50 seconds at HIGH (100%).

Easy!

1 pound ground beef
¼ cup chopped onion
1 package dry taco mix
¼ cup catsup
10½-ounce can tomato
  soup

1½ teaspoons chili powder
15-ounce can kidney
  beans with liquid,
  mashed
shredded cheddar cheese
  for garnish

1. Microwave ground beef and onion in a 1½-quart casserole for 4 to 5 minutes at HIGH (100%) until meat is no longer pink. Drain off fat.

2. Stir in remaining ingredients. Microwave for 5 to 6 minutes at MEDIUM HIGH (70%) until bubbly. Garnish with shredded cheese. Serve hot with taco or corn chips or taco shells.

Yields: 8 to 12 servings.

MOZZARELLA AND GARLIC
FRENCH BREAD

———— · · · · · ————

A favorite appetizer or accompaniment to any meal.

1 loaf French bread
¼ cup butter, soft
garlic salt

1 cup shredded
　mozzarella cheese
½ cup Parmesan cheese
　(optional)

1. Slice French bread. Butter every other slice liberally and sprinkle with garlic salt, mozzarella cheese, and Parmesan cheese.

2. Microwave only half of loaf at a time. Wrap in original paper wrapper (not foil) or in paper toweling. Microwave for 1 to 2 minutes at MEDIUM (50%) or until cheese is melted and bread is warmed.

Yields: 8 to 10 servings.

———— · ❄ · ————

Compacts: Microwave for 1 to 1½ minutes at HIGH (100%) in step #2.

TIPS

· · · · ·

Wrapping the bread in paper toweling prevents it from becoming soggy while microwaving. A plain wicker or woven basket is microwave-safe for a short cooking time, so I often microwave the loaf in a long narrow basket lined with napkins that wrap around the loaf.

BACON STICK APPETIZERS

———— · · · · · ————

12 bread sticks (½ inch
　diameter), garlic,
　onion, or plain flavored
6–12 slices bacon

¼ cup Parmesan cheese
Parmesan cheese for
　garnish

1. Slice bacon in half lengthwise. Wrap one or two slices of bacon around each bread stick, spiral fashion. Roll in Parmesan cheese.

Use the baked and crisp bread sticks that are usually located near the cracker section of your grocery store. Bacon Stick Appetizers look very attractive when served in a large colorful mug at a casual get-together.

2. Place on a paper plate or dish that has been lined with a paper towel.

3. Microwave 6 at a time for 4 to 5 minutes at HIGH (100%) until crisp. Sprinkle with Parmesan cheese. Serve in a decorative cup or glass.

Yields: 12 appetizers.

———————— · ❄ · ————————

PIZZA BAGLETS OR CANAPÉS

———————— · · · · · ————————

Tasty and easy.

½ cup ketchup
1½ teaspoons Italian
   seasoning
24 split baglets (12 whole
   miniature bagels = 24
   split baglets)

½ cup browned
   hamburger, sausage, or
   chopped pepperoni
½ cup mozzarella cheese
¼ cup Parmesan cheese

1. Mix ketchup with Italian seasoning. Spread on each baglet. Top each with meat; sprinkle with mozzarella, then sprinkle with Parmesan cheese.

2. Place on a paper towel or paper plate. Microwave 8 at a time for 1 to 1½ minutes at MEDIUM HIGH (70%) or until cheese is melted and filling is heated. Serve immediately.

Yields: 24 servings.

———————— · ❄ · ————————

Variation: Add any or all of the following with the meat: ½ cup chopped green onion, ¼ cup sliced mushrooms, ¼ cup black olives, ¼ cup chopped green pepper. You may also substitute English muffins or buns for the baglets. Top and slice into quarters.

CHICKEN OR BEEF KABOBS

. . . . .

Delicious appetizers or party snacks.

3 tablespoons soy sauce
1½ teaspoons brown sugar
½ teaspoon garlic salt
dash ginger
¾–1 pound deboned and
   skinned chicken or 1
   pound sirloin or tender
   steak, cut into cubes

1 green pepper, cut into
   ½-inch cubes or 15-
   ounce can pineapple
   chunks
12–15 mushrooms,
   washed and cut in half
1 tablespoon honey

1. Mix soy sauce, sugar, garlic salt, and ginger for marinade. Stir in chicken or steak. Refrigerate for 15 minutes or until needed.

2. Drain chicken or steak, reserving marinade. Alternate pepper or pineapple chunks, chicken or steak, and mushrooms on round wooden picks.

3. Stir honey into reserved marinade. Brush each kabob generously with the marinade. Microwave kabobs on a paper plate or towel for 4 to 7 minutes at HIGH (100%) until meat is done and tender. Baste after 2 minutes with marinade. Rotate dish once during microwaving if necessary for even cooking.

Yields: 25 to 30 kabobs.

❋

T I P S

. . . . .

Long wooden skewers may be used instead of round cocktail picks as they will hold twice as much of the cubed food. Two or three skewers may be served with cooked rice to make a tasty entrée.

The flavors blend well if cocktail balls and sauce are microwaved in advance and refrigerated, then reheated before serving.

Heat-and-serve sausage links may be substituted for the meatballs for an even quicker appetizer. Cut links into thirds and proceed with step #2.

COCKTAIL MEATBALLS
IN ITALIAN SAUCE

——— · · · · · ———

Especially good (and easy too) when served with mozzarella and Garlic French Bread (see page 26) for evening hors d'oeuvres.

1 pound sausage
1 egg
½ package dry onion soup
   mix
Micro Shake or natural
   browning powder
   (optional)

16-ounce jar spicy
   spaghetti sauce
½ cup Parmesan or
   Romano cheese

1. Combine sausage, egg, and soup mix. Shape into 1-inch balls on a roasting rack or paper plate. Sprinkle with Micro Shake. Cover loosely with waxed paper. Microwave for 7 to 9 minutes at HIGH (100%) until meatballs are no longer pink, stirring twice. Drain off fat.

2. Combine spaghetti sauce and sausage balls in a 1½-quart casserole. Microwave for 7 to 10 minutes at MEDIUM HIGH (70%) until sauce thickens slightly and flavors are absorbed by sausage balls. Serve in a chafing dish garnished with Parmesan cheese (with a dispenser of cocktail picks nearby).

Yields: 8 to 10 servings.

——— · ❄ · ———

Compacts: Follow the same recipe and times using HIGH (100%) instead of using MEDIUM HIGH (70%).

BEVERAGES

· ❄ ·

WARM CITRUS APPETIZER

· · · · ·

1 cup pineapple juice
1½ cups cranberry juice
1½ cups hot water

3 cups orange juice
1½ tablespoons lemon
   juice

1. Combine all the ingredients in a 2-quart bowl.

2. Microwave for 11 to 12 minutes at HIGH (100%) or 160°F. Serve hot in glass mugs garnished with a thin orange slice.

Yields: 8 to 10 servings.

· ❄ ·

SPICY HOT CIDER OR WASSAIL

· · · · ·

15 cloves
1 lemon, sliced thin
1 orange, sliced thin
1 or 2 quarts apple cider

½ teaspoon allspice
2 tablespoons brown
   sugar
2 cinnamon sticks

1. Put 1 clove in the center of each orange or lemon slice. Set aside.

2. Combine remaining ingredients in a 2- or 3-quart bowl, depending on amount of cider used. Mix well. Add fruit slices.

T I P S
· · · · ·
Warm Citrus Appetizer is a pretty red color so it is especially appropriate for holiday entertaining.

Traditional wassail recipes include beer or ale instead of the orange juice, so this is a tasty nonalcoholic version. The clove-studded orange and lemon slices floating in either the cider or wassail give the beverage even more eye and taste appeal.

3. Microwave for 10 or 15 minutes at HIGH (100%) or until hot and bubbly (160°F.). Serve warm with fruit slices floating in the cups.

Yields: 5 to 10 servings.

—————— · ❄ · ——————

Variation: For wassail, use 2 quarts apple cider. In addition to the ingredients listed above, add ½ cup lemon juice, 2 cups orange juice, and ¾ cup white sugar. A dash of nutmeg is optional. Proceed as directed.

CRANBERRY-LEMON PUNCH

—————— · · • · · ——————

Great for the party after Christmas caroling or a holiday get-together!

10 cloves
1 lemon, sliced thin
2½ cups cranberry juice
6-ounce can frozen
   lemonade concentrate

1 cinnamon stick
1¼ cups water

1. Put 1 clove in the center of each lemon slice.
2. Combine remaining ingredients in a 2-quart microwave pitcher. Mix well. Add lemon slices.
3. Microwave for 8 to 10 minutes at HIGH (100%) or until 155°F. Serve warm with lemon slices.

Yields: 5 to 6 servings.

—————— · ❄ · ——————

· ·

Everyone should hear a little music, read a little poetry, and see a fine picture every day of his life, so that he does not lose the sense of the beauty that God has planted in the human soul.

BREADS

· · · · ·

· **Microwaved breads do not brown.** To create an attractive appearance on the top, brush with butter or milk and sprinkle with one of the following before microwaving:

> Bread, cake, or cracker crumbs
> Cinnamon and sugar
> Parmesan cheese and/or poppy seed
> Oatmeal, cornmeal, or crushed cereal

· **Microwave muffin batter in 2 paper liners** (one will absorb the moisture) **for 25 to 30 seconds at HIGH (100%).** For 6 muffins, microwave for 2½ minutes at HIGH (100%).

· **For bread, always use a microwave-safe bread or tube pan that has been greased with oil** (or sprayed with shortening) **and dusted with sugar. DO NOT DUST WITH FLOUR** because the bread will stick and be difficult to remove from the pan if you do.

· If the bottom of microwaved bread tends not to cook in your microwave oven, **place bread in the pan on an inverted pie plate** so microwaves can easily reach the bottom.

· When using a microwave loaf pan, **shield edges 1 to 1½ inches with foil to prevent ends and corners from overcooking before the center is done.** Remove foil for the last half of the microwaving time.

· **Microwave quick nut-type breads for 7 to 9 minutes at MEDIUM HIGH (70%).** Stand 5 minutes.

· **If sensitive ingredients such as cheese, cream cheese, sour cream, and/or large amounts of fruit** are used in a quick-bread recipe, **microwave for 9 minutes at MEDIUM (50%) and then again for 2 to 5 minutes at HIGH (100%).** Stand 5 minutes.

· **Bread will be done when** a toothpick inserted near the center of the bread comes out clean.

· **To proof or quickly "rise" dough:** Cover with plastic wrap. Microwave for 1 minute at MEDIUM (50%). Let rest 10 to 15 minutes. Repeat 1 to 2 times. Uncover before baking.

· **Microwave yeast breads for 10 to 13 minutes at MEDIUM (50%) with edges shielded 1 to 1½** inches. Remove foil for last half of cooking time. **Microwave 2 loaves for 13 to 16 minutes at MEDIUM (50%) with edges shielded as directed above.**

Six-ounce custard cups work well if you do not have a microwave muffin pan. Be sure to arrange them in a circle to ensure even cooking. Remember to use two cupcake liners per muffin because the liners prevent the muffins from becoming soggy on the bottom. Throw away the outside liner before serving.

Children will enjoy microwaving a single muffin for breakfast from the ready-made batter.

RAISIN BRAN MUFFINS
(WITH BRAN AND DATE VARIATION)

————— . . . . . —————

The batter will keep in your refrigerator for 4 to 5 weeks, so enjoy a few hot muffins every night.

1 cup hot water	2 eggs
3 cups Raisin Bran cereal	2 cups buttermilk
½ cup butter or	2½ cups flour
margarine, soft	2 teaspoons baking soda
1½ cups sugar	

1. Microwave the hot water in a 1-quart bowl for 1 to 2 minutes at HIGH (100%) until boiling. Add bran cereal. Set aside.

2. Mix butter and sugar well. Beat in eggs and buttermilk. Mix (or sift together) flour and soda. Add to buttermilk mixture. Blend well.

3. Stir the buttermilk mixture into the bran mixture. Store in a tightly covered container in your refrigerator.

To cook muffins: Spoon batter into muffin or custard cups that have been lined with 2 paper baking cups. Fill ½ to ⅔ full. For 1 muffin: Microwave for 25 to 30 seconds at HIGH (100%). For 2 muffins: Microwave for 1 minute at HIGH (100%). For 4 muffins: Microwave for 1½ to 2 minutes at HIGH (100%). For 6 muffins: Microwave for 2½ to 3 minutes at HIGH (100%).

Yields: 36 to 40 muffins.

————— · ❄ · —————

Optional topping: Sprinkle with this mixture before baking: 1 tablespoon crushed graham crackers, 1 tablespoon sugar, and ¼ teaspoon cinnamon.

Variation: For bran muffins, substitute 3 cups All-Bran cereal for the Raisin Bran in step #1. Add 1 cup chopped dates or raisins in step #3.

EASY CORN BREAD RING

————— · · · · · —————

¼ cup butter	¾ cup cornmeal
¼ cup sugar	1 teaspoon baking powder
2 eggs	½ teaspoon salt
1 cup milk	3 tablespoons crushed
1 cup flour	cornflakes or cereal

1. Microwave butter in a mixing bowl for 30 seconds at HIGH (100%) until melted. Beat in sugar, eggs, and milk. Mix dry ingredients and stir into egg mixture until smooth.

2. Pour batter into a buttered ring pan that has been sprinkled with crushed cornflakes.

3. Place in oven on an inverted saucer.

4. Microwave for 5 to 7 minutes at MEDIUM HIGH (70%) until no longer doughy. Let stand 2 minutes. Invert onto serving plate.

Yields: 1 ring (6 to 8 servings).

————— · ❄ · —————

Compacts: Microwave at HIGH (100%) instead of MEDIUM HIGH.

TIPS
· · · ·

Using a microwave ring pan will prevent the corners from overcooking. A 5-cup ring is the best size.

I created this recipe while
trying to lose a few pounds
on a very low-calorie
diet—NO FLOUR! NO
SUGAR! The zucchini and
apple provide bulk. I
found these muffins quite
tasty when I was trying to
live without bread and
butter.

LOW-CALORIE BRAN MUFFINS

· · · · ·

No flour in this recipe; for diet food, they taste great!

1 small unpeeled zucchini
   squash, washed and
   grated to ½ cup
1 large unpeeled apple,
   washed, cored, and
   grated to 1 cup
1 teaspoon vanilla
2 eggs
½ teaspoon nutmeg

1 teaspoon cinnamon
½ teaspoon soda
1 teaspoon baking powder
1 teaspoon lemon juice
low-calorie sugar
   substitute (or fructose)
   equal to ⅓ cup sugar (8
   packets)
1 cup unprocessed bran

1. In a food processor bowl, blender container, or mixing bowl combine all ingredients except the bran.

2. Add the bran and blend well using the food processor, blender, or mixer.

3. Spoon batter into paper-lined muffin cups (of a microwave muffin pan) or custard cups. Fill ½ to ⅔ full.

4. Microwave at **MEDIUM** (50%) for 3½ minutes.

5. Then microwave at **HIGH** (100%) for 1 to 2 minutes to finish cooking. (Muffins will be very moist.)

Yields: 10 to 12 muffins (35 calories per muffin).

———— · ❄ · ————

· ·

Kindness is the golden chain by which society is bound together.

NUTRITIOUS ENGLISH MUFFIN BREAD
WITH RAISINS

———— · · · · · ————

*This is a delicious no-knead bread that is made to be
sliced and toasted.*

1½ cups white flour	½ teaspoons baking soda
3 cups whole wheat flour	2 packages dry yeast
½ cup rye flour	2½ cups 2% low-fat milk
½ cup brown sugar	cornmeal
1½ teaspoons salt	1 cup raisins

1. Set aside 1 cup of the white flour. Using a food processor
or mixer, combine the remaining 4 cups of flours, sugar, soda,
salt, and yeast.

2. Microwave low-fat milk in a 1-quart bowl for 3 minutes
at HIGH (100%) or until 130°F. Add slowly to dry mixture,
beating well.

3. Beat in remaining 1 cup of flour and raisins.

4. Pour into 2 microwave loaf pans that have been greased
and dusted with cornmeal.

5. Allow dough to rise, covered, for 40 to 50 minutes in a
warm place, or for speed rise, microwave for 1 minute at ME-
DIUM (50%) covered with plastic wrap. Let stand 10 minutes. Repeat once.

6. Uncover. Sprinkle with cornmeal. Microwave each loaf
with corners shielded for 6 minutes at MEDIUM HIGH
(70%). Remove foil and microwave again for 2 to 2½ minutes
at MEDIUM HIGH (70%). Rotate dish once if necessary for
even cooking.

7. Let stand 5 minutes before removing from pans.

Yields: 2 loaves.

———— · ❄ · ————

Compacts: Microwave for 5 minutes at HIGH (100%).

Our favorite breakfast
bread! I often use 5 cups of
whole wheat flour as this
adds more fiber to the al-
ready low-fat recipe.

To ensure the bottom of
the loaf will cook evenly,
place the pan on an in-
verted saucer in the microwave oven so the micro-
waves will bounce off the
floor of the oven and cook
the bottom side.

Remove foil shielding and microwave again for 2 to 3 minutes at HIGH (100%) in step #6.

Variation: For English muffin date bread, omit raisins or substitute dates. Substitute all white flour or wheat-blend flour or any flours to make 5 cups.

T I P S
· · · · ·

To prevent fruit and nuts from sinking to the bottom while microwaving, coat fruit and nuts with 1 tablespoon additional flour before stirring them into the batter.

If the bottoms of baked products undercook in your microwave oven, place your filled loaf pan on an inverted saucer or pie plate during microwaving. This will allow the microwaves to bounce off the bottom of your oven and then cook the bottom of the food.

PUMPKIN BREAD OR ZUCCHINI BREAD

· · · · ·

½ cup brown sugar (packed)	½ teaspoon baking powder
½ cup butter, soft	½ teaspoon salt
2 eggs, beaten	1 teaspoon cinnamon
1 cup cooked or canned pumpkin	⅓ cup chopped nuts
1¼ cups flour	½ cup raisins or chopped dates
½ teaspoon baking soda	¼ cup chopped maraschino cherries

1. Cream or blend brown sugar and butter. Beat in eggs and pumpkin. Mix dry ingredients well. Add to egg mixture. Blend well. Stir in nuts, raisins, and cherries.

2. Pour into a greased and sugared ring mold or loaf pan. Shield corners of loaf pan. (Sprinkle with cinnamon and sugar topping if desired or other topping; see Blender Banana Bread, on page 41.)

*3. Microwave for 8 to 10 minutes at MEDIUM HIGH (70%). Stand 10 minutes before removing from pan.

Yields: 1 loaf.

———— · ❄ · ————

Compacts: Microwave for 8 to 10 minutes at HIGH (100%) in step #3.

Variation: For zucchini bread, substitute 1¼ cups grated, unpared zucchini for the 1 cup cooked pumpkin.

· ·
*Rotate pan once, if necessary, for even cooking.

ALMOND BUTTER BRUNCH BUBBLE

· · · · ·

Use your convection microwave or your range with your microwave.

½ cup butter (butter works better than margarine)
1 cup brown sugar
¼ cup chopped maraschino cherries

½ cup sliced almonds or ¾ cup chopped pecans
2 large (12-ounce) tubes refrigerated buttermilk biscuits

1. Combine butter and brown sugar in a 2-cup measure. Microwave for 1½ to 2 minutes at HIGH (100%) or until boiling. Stir to make a syrup.

2. Pour ½ of the syrup in the bottom of a bundt pan. Sprinkle on the cherries and the almonds, reserving a few almonds for the top. Stand biscuits on edge around the pan. Cover top with remaining syrup and the few almonds.

3. **Convection microwave (LOW-MIX):** Bake at 350° or Combination #2 or Code #2 for 25 minutes. Cool 5 minutes. Invert and serve.

For a microwave and a conventional oven: Use a microwave- and oven-safe bundt pan. Preheat your conventional oven to 400°F. Bake for 20 minutes; then microwave for 5 minutes at MEDIUM HIGH (70%). Cool 5 minutes. Invert and serve.

Yields: 10 to 12 servings.

—— · ❄ · ——

· ·
A smile is a curve that can set a lot of things straight.

Be sure to use brand-name biscuits because generic biscuits taste salty (I prefer Pillsbury or Big Country or Hungry Jack). Three 8-ounce tubes of biscuits may be substituted for the two large 12-ounce tubes.

Choose the convection microwave setting in step #3 that corresponds to the one on your convection microwave oven.

Don't worry if you don't have a convection microwave. This recipe works just as well using your conventional oven and your microwave. Be sure to use an oven-safe and microwave-safe bundt pan.

The blender speeds mixing. What could be easier to make? A food processor works even better.

Chopped walnuts or pecans work well in this delicious bread.

For ease in slicing, wrap loaf in plastic wrap and refrigerate overnight. Unwrap and slice while still chilled.

Shielding corners with foil for half the microwaving time (7 minutes) will help keep the corners from even slightly overcooking if you are using a loaf pan.

BLENDER BANANA BREAD

· · · · ·

Use your blender or food processor!

· BLEND #1 ·

2 eggs
½ cup brown sugar
⅓ cup white sugar
⅓ cup vegetable oil

2 ripe bananas (large),
  sliced
¼ cup buttermilk
1 teaspoon vanilla

· BLEND #2 ·

1¾ cups flour (½ may be
  wheat flour)
¼ teaspoon baking
  powder

1 teaspoon baking soda
½ teaspoon salt

Add:
½ cup chopped nuts

· TOPPING ·

¼ cup flour
2 tablespoons brown
  sugar

1 teaspoon cinnamon
1 tablespoon butter, soft

1. Blend all the #1 ingredients in your blender for 10 seconds.

2. Sift all the #2 ingredients into the blender. Blend 2 to 3 seconds only, to mix with the #1 ingredients. Add nuts.

3. Pour into a greased and sugared loaf pan or ring dish.

4. Mix topping ingredients (or use ⅓ cup crushed graham crackers). Sprinkle on top. Place in microwave on an inverted saucer.

5. Microwave for 10 minutes at MEDIUM (50%). Rotate dish one-half turn. Microwave again for 3 to 4 minutes at HIGH (100%). Let stand 10 minutes before removing from pan.   Yields: 1 loaf.

· ❄ ·

Compacts: Microwave for 8 to 10 minutes at HIGH (100%) in step #5.

EASY WHOLE-WHEAT BATTER BREAD

────── · · · · · ──────

(Or White Bread Variation)

1½ cups very warm water (110°F.)
1 package yeast
3 tablespoons brown sugar

1 cup whole wheat flour
2 cups white flour
1 teaspoon salt
¼ cup oil

1. Dissolve yeast in water in a 2-quart bowl. Set aside for 5 minutes. Stir in brown sugar. Add the remaining ingredients. Beat thoroughly; cover.

2. Microwave for 1 minute at MEDIUM (50%) Rest 15 minutes. Repeat until batter has doubled.

3. Stir down batter. Place in an oiled 9-inch pie plate or ring pan. Cover and microwave for 1 minute at MEDIUM (50%). Rest 15 minutes. Repeat.

4. Brush with milk and sprinkle with oatmeal if desired. Microwave uncovered for 12 to 15 minutes at MEDIUM (50%). Invert immediately.

Yields: 1 loaf.

────── · ❄ · ──────

Compacts: Microwave for 8 to 9 minutes at HIGH (100%) in step #4. Proof (or rise) bread without microwaving in step #2 and #3.

Variation: For white batter bread: Use all white flour and substitute white sugar for the brown sugar.

One advantage of microwaving bread is the time saved. By using the microwave oven you can even cut the proofing time for conventionally baked bread by one half. Be sure to microwave at MEDIUM (50%) for only 1 minute and then allow the bread to rest (stand in the microwave oven) for 15 minutes to allow the bread to rise. Repeat one time for most doughs.

TIPS
· · · · ·

Microwave Caramel Rolls may also become Refrigerator Rolls: Refrigerate rolls overnight after step #2 and omit step #3.

For Quick Browned Rolls: Combine your regular oven with your microwave oven. Preheat oven to 350°. Follow directions through step #3. Omit step #4, and bake rolls for 30 minutes at 350°.

From freezer to table in 35 minutes or less.

½ cup brown sugar
¼ cup butter
½ (3-ounce) package butterscotch pudding mix (¼ cup), not instant

½ cup chopped pecans, sliced almonds, or chopped nuts
12 frozen dough rolls

1. Microwave butter and brown sugar in a small bowl for 1 to 2 minutes at HIGH (100%) until bubbly. Stir in pudding mix. Set aside.

2. Butter a 9-inch ring mold or pie plate. Sprinkle with chopped nuts. Place rolls in dish. Pour pudding-syrup over rolls. Cover with plastic wrap.

3. Microwave rolls for 8 to 9 minutes at LOW (10%) until rolls are thawed but not heated. Stand 20 minutes until doubled in size.

4. Remove plastic wrap. Cover with a paper towel or napkin. Microwave for 6 to 7½ minutes at MEDIUM (50%) until an impression can no longer be left in the dough when touched gently. Let stand 5 minutes. Invert.

Yields: 12 rolls.

─────── · ❄ · ───────

Variation: For caramel buns: Substitute 2 cans refrigerated biscuits for the rolls and cut each biscuit into quarters; substitute 1 tablespoon orange juice concentrate for the pudding mix. Follow recipe as listed, omitting step #3 (biscuits do not need to rise).

CANDIES

· · · · ·

· Candy-making in the microwave will reduce cooking time by 75 percent.

· Always use a large 2-quart microwave-safe bowl as ingredients will "bubble or boil up" more than on your range top.

· Do not use a regular candy thermometer while microwaving. It will not work but will most likely break and shatter. (You can insert it immediately after cooking to test the temperature.)

· You can use a special microwave thermometer that is made for microwaving candy syrups. (See order blank in back of book or check with your microwave accessory shop.)

· To test candy for doneness, drop a small amount into a small cup of very cold water and then form into a ball:

Soft ball (234°–240°F.) will flatten when removed from the water.

Firm ball (244°–248°F.) will not flatten but will be rounded when removed from the water.

Hard ball (250°–266°F.) will be very firm yet pliable when removed from the water.

· **No change in ingredients is needed** for microwaving candies using conventional recipes (as long as smaller recipes are used).

· **Do not use margarine that remains soft when refrigerated.** Some microwave candies will not "set up" with this type of shortening.

MICROWAVE CHERRY MASH CANDY

· · · · ·

12 large marshmallows
2 cups sugar
dash of salt
⅔ cup evaporated milk
½ cup butter
10-ounce package cherry
  chips

2 cups (12 ounces) choco-
  late chips, milk choco-
  late or semisweet
⅔ cup peanut butter
1 pound salted blanched
  peanuts, chopped

1. Combine marshmallows, sugar, salt, milk, and butter in a 2-quart bowl. Microwave for 4 to 5 minutes at HIGH (100%) until mixture boils. Microwave again for 4 minutes at MEDIUM (50%), stirring 2 or 3 times.

2. Add cherry chips and stir until melted. Pour into a 9x13-inch buttered pan. Chill until firm.

3. Combine chocolate chips and peanut butter in a 2-quart bowl. Microwave for 2 to 3 minutes at HIGH (100%). Stir until melted and smooth. Stir in peanuts.

4. Pour over cherry layer. Chill until firm. Cut into squares.

Yields: 4 to 5 dozen pieces.

· ❄ ·

Compacts: Microwave for 6 to 8 minutes at HIGH (100%) instead of total time in step #1.

3-MINUTE MICROWAVE FUDGE

· · · · ·

1 pound powdered sugar
   (3¾ cups)
½ cup cocoa
1 stick margarine (½ cup)

¼ cup milk
1 teaspoon vanilla
½ cup chopped peanuts
   (dry roasted)

1. Combine powdered sugar and cocoa in a 2-quart microwave-safe bowl.

2. Place the stick of margarine on top of the mixture. Pour the milk over all. Do not stir!

3. Microwave at HIGH (100%) for 3 minutes.

4. Stir well and add the vanilla and peanuts.

5. Pour into a greased 8x8-inch pan. Cool 20 minutes. Cut into squares.

Yields: 64 pieces.

· ❄ ·

TIPS

· · · · ·

Make sure you use a margarine that is solid at room temperature so that the fudge will set up.

For an even richer fudge: Substitute evaporated milk or half-and-half for the milk in step #2.

A microwave corn popper is an inexpensive accessory that will allow you to pop bulk popcorn in your microwave oven in about 3 minutes.

The prepackaged microwave popcorn is often high in sodium and cholesterol so read the package before you buy.

When popping corn in the microwave popper or a prepackaged bag, turn the microwave off when popping slows to one or two seconds between pops. Do NOT expect all the kernels to pop. If you wait for that, the rest of the popcorn will be scorched.

LIGHT CARAMEL CORN
(MADE IN A GROCERY SACK)

_____ · · · · · _____

It's light, tasty, and easy—and cleanup is a breeze!

3 quarts popcorn (popped) *	**⅓ cup corn syrup**
½ cup butter or margarine	**dash of salt**
⅔ cup light brown sugar	**1 teaspoon baking soda**

1. Place popped popcorn in a paper grocery bag and roll up ends tightly for ease in handling later. Unroll. Set aside.

2. Microwave butter, sugar, syrup, and salt in a 2-quart bowl for 2 to 3 minutes at HIGH (100%) or until boiling. Stir. Microwave again for 2 minutes at HIGH (100%), stirring often.

3. Stir in soda. Pour over popped corn in the bag. Roll up ends. Microwave for 2 minutes at HIGH (100%). Shake well in bag. Microwave again for 1 minute at HIGH (100%). Pour onto waxed paper or foil. Enjoy!

Yields: 3 quarts.

_____ · ❈ · _____

. . . .
*Pop corn in a microwave corn popper or on the range or use microwave popcorn. Do not pop the corn in a plain paper bag as that could result in a fire.

CHOCOLATE TURTLES

——— · · · · · ———

Delicious—tastes like $16.00 per pound.

2 cups chocolate chips
2 tablespoons shortening
14-ounce package
  caramels

⅓ cup margarine or butter
2 tablespoons milk
1 cup whole pecan halves

1. Microwave chocolate chips and shortening in a 2-quart bowl for 2 to 3 minutes at MEDIUM HIGH (70%).

2. Pour only half of the melted chocolate into a foil-lined 8-inch pan. Refrigerate 15 minutes.

3. Microwave caramels, margarine, and milk in a 1-quart bowl for 4 to 5 minutes at MEDIUM HIGH (70%). Stir in pecans. Pour over refrigerated chocolate.

4. Reheat remaining chocolate mixture for 1 minute at MEDIUM HIGH (70%). Spread chocolate over caramel layer. Refrigerate 1 to 1½ hours. Invert pan. Peel foil. Cut into 1-inch squares. Store in the refrigerator.

Yields: 5 dozen candies.

——— · · ———

Keep these delicious morsels refrigerated until serving time. They will become sticky if kept in a warm room for more than an hour.

CARAMELS

· · · · ·

A microwave candy ther-
mometer is especially
helpful to determine when
the caramel mixture
reaches the hard ball
stage.

If mixture separates
while cooking, beat until
smooth with a beater.

2 cups sugar

1 cup whipping cream

5 tablespoons butter

⅔ cup corn syrup

dash of salt

⅔ cup whipping cream

1½ teaspoons vanilla

1 cup walnut or pecan
halves

1. Microwave the sugar, 1 cup cream, butter, syrup, and salt in a 2-quart bowl for 11 to 12 minutes at HIGH (100%), stirring three times. Stir in the ⅔ cup cream.

2. Microwave again for 10 to 12 minutes at MEDIUM HIGH (70%) or until a firm ball (248° F.) forms when a small amount is dropped in cold water, stirring 3 times.

3. Stir in vanilla and nuts. Pour into a buttered and foil-lined 8-inch square pan. Cool until firm. Invert. Peel off foil. Cut into 1-inch squares. Wrap in plastic wrap.

Yields: 3 dozen candies.

· ❄ ·

OLD-FASHIONED DIVINITY

· · · · ·

*Tastes like mother used to make, but takes only half
the time.*

2½ cups sugar	2 large egg whites
½ cup light corn syrup	1 teaspoon vanilla
½ cup water	½ cup chopped nuts or
dash of salt	cherries (optional)

1. Combine sugar, syrup, water, and salt in a 2-quart microwave bowl. Cover with plastic wrap.

2. Microwave for 5 minutes at HIGH (100%). Stir.

3. Microwave again, uncovered this time, for 12 to 13 minutes at HIGH (100%) until a hard ball (258° F.) forms when a small amount is dropped in cold water. Cool 5 minutes.

4. Beat egg whites until very stiff using an upright mixer. Pour syrup over egg whites, beating constantly until mixture starts to lose its gloss. Beat in vanilla and nuts and continue beating until candy will hold its shape. Drop by teaspoonfuls onto waxed paper.

Yields: 3 dozen candies.

· ·

TIPS
· · · · ·

Colorful and flavorful divinity may be created by beating 2 to 3 tablespoons flavored gelatin (like Jello) into the stiffly beaten egg whites in step #4 (before pouring in the syrup).

In step #4 beat only until mixture starts to lose its gloss (about 8 to 10 minutes). Divinity will become too stiff if beaten too long but will not set up if underbeaten.

TIPS
· · · · ·

This is our family's favorite fudge recipe, handed down from our dear aunt. Just remember to microwave for 4 minutes beyond boiling.

3 cups sugar
1 tablespoon water
5½-ounce can (⅔ cup) evaporated milk
1 stick (½ cup) margarine
2 cups (12 ounces) chocolate chips

7-ounce jar marshmallow creme
1 cup chopped nuts (optional)
1 teaspoon vanilla

1. In a 2-quart bowl, combine the sugar, water, milk, and margarine. Microwave for 3½ to 4½ minutes at HIGH (100%) until mixture boils.

2. Microwave again for 4 minutes at MEDIUM HIGH (70%), stirring twice.

3. Stir in chocolate chips until they are melted.

4. Stir in marshmallow creme, nuts, and vanilla.

5. Pour into a greased 9x13-inch pan.

6. Cool at least 15 minutes. Cut into squares.

Yields: 6 to 8 dozen pieces.

CORRINNE'S FUDGE-SCOTCH SQUARES

—— · · · · · ——

Delicious and so easy when a few dozen bars are needed!

1½ cups graham cracker
   crumbs
14-ounce can sweetened
   condensed milk

1 cup chocolate chips
1 cup butterscotch chips
1 cup chopped nuts

1. Combine all ingredients. Press into a 9-inch square pan. Shield corners with foil.

2. Microwave for 5 minutes at HIGH (100%). Remove foil shielding. Microwave for 1 to 2½ minutes longer at MEDIUM HIGH (70%).

3. Chill ½ hour. Cut into squares. Dust with powdered sugar.

Yields: 3 dozen squares.

—— · ❄ · ——

. . . .

Though we travel the world over to find the beautiful, we must carry it with us or we will not find it.

These bars appear very moist after cooking, but they become firm when cooled and separated for serving.

Sweet milk chocolate chips work best in this recipe.

ROCKY ROAD FUDGE

———— · · · · · ————

Fast, easy, and delicious.

2 cups chocolate chips
¼ cup butter or margarine
2 tablespoons shortening

5 cups miniature marsh-
   mallows (10½-ounce
   bag)
½ cup chopped peanuts

1. Combine chocolate chips, butter, and shortening in a 2-quart bowl.
2. Microwave for 2 to 3 minutes at MEDIUM HIGH (70%) until chips are soft. Stir until smooth.
3. Stir in marshmallows and peanuts. Spread evenly into a buttered 8-inch pan.
4. Refrigerate until firm. Cut into squares.

Yields: 64 1-inch squares.

———— · · ————

9-MINUTE PEANUT BRITTLE

—— · · · · · ——

No need for raw peanuts in this recipe.
You'll be surprised at how good this is in such
a short time!

1 cup sugar
½ cup light corn syrup
1 cup dry roasted salted
  peanuts

1 teaspoon butter
1 teaspoon vanilla
1 teaspoon baking soda

1. Butter a 12-inch or larger cookie sheet or tray. Set aside.

2. Combine sugar and corn syrup in a 2-quart bowl. Microwave for 4 minutes at HIGH (100%).

3. Stir in peanuts. Microwave again for 4 to 5 minutes, until light brown, at HIGH (100%).

4. Add butter and vanilla. Blend. Microwave again for 30 to 60 seconds at HIGH (100%).

5. Add baking soda and gently stir until well mixed and foamy. Pour onto buttered cookie sheet. Cool ½ hour. Break into pieces.

Yields: 1 pound candy.

—— · ❄ · ——

Variation: For coconut-pecan brittle, substitute ¾ cup pecan halves and ¾ cup coconut for peanuts in step #3 as directed.

I prefer using dry roasted peanuts in this recipe, but you may also use raw peanuts. If you do, add the raw peanuts to the sugar–corn syrup mixture in step #2 before microwaving. In step #3 just stir and continue to microwave.

Make sure peanut-syrup mixture turns brown in step #3 before adding the butter. The darker the color, the more it will be brittle and taste of "burnt sugar," which is often desirable, like the "original" old-fashioned taste.

Try butterscotch or mint flavorings.

----- · · · · · -----

½ cup corn syrup
1 cup sugar
¼ cup water
few drops food coloring
   (optional)

½ teaspoon flavoring
   (orange, strawberry, or
   peppermint extract,
   etc.)
10 wooden popsicle sticks

1. Microwave syrup, sugar and water for 10 to 13 minutes at HIGH (100%) to hard-crack stage (310°F.). Stir in flavoring and coloring.

2. Pour over sticks arranged on buttered foil. Cool until hardened.

To form perfectly rounded lollipops: Make molds by cutting 1 inch off the top of wax-coated drinking cups. Punch a small hole in the side of the 1-inch piece, inserting the stick. Pour lollipop mixture into molds on buttered foil.

Yields: 10 lollipops.

----- · ❄ · -----

PEANUT BUTTER BARS

— · · · · · —

1 cup peanut butter
2 sticks butter or
  margarine (1 cup)
1¾ cups graham cracker
  crumbs
2½ cups powdered sugar
  (do not sift)

2 cups (12 ounces)
  chocolate chips
  semisweet or sweet
2 tablespoons butter or
  margarine

1. Place peanut butter and the 2 sticks of butter in a 2-quart bowl.

2. Microwave for 30 to 40 seconds at HIGH (100%) until very soft but not melted. Stir.

3. Mix in the cracker crumbs and the powdered sugar.

4. Press mixture into a 9x13-inch cake pan or a 10½x15-inch jelly roll pan.

5. Combine the chocolate chips and the 2 tablespoons of butter with the peanut butter mixture. Microwave for 2½ minutes at MEDIUM HIGH (70%) or until melted. Stir until smooth and quickly spread over bars. Refrigerate until almost firm (½ hour) and cut into bars. Keep refrigerated.

Yields: 6 to 8 dozen bars.

— · ❄ · —

· ·

Making excuses doesn't change the truth.

TIPS

· · · ·

Keep these delicious bars refrigerated until serving time. They will become sticky if kept in a warm room for more than an hour.

TIPS

. . . .

Remove syrup when it reaches exactly 230°F. in step #2. If the syrup overcooks in step #2, the candy will become crumbly.

. . . . .

2 cups sugar
⅔ cup milk
1 teaspoon vanilla

½ teaspoon burnt-sugar flavoring
1 cup marshmallow creme
1 cup peanut butter

1. Combine sugar and milk in a 3-quart microwave bowl. Microwave for 3 minutes at HIGH (100%). Stir.

2. Microwave again for 8 minutes at MEDIUM HIGH (70%) or until a soft ball forms (230°F.) when a small amount is dropped in cold water.

3. Stir in the flavorings, marshmallow creme, and peanut butter.

4. Pour into a buttered 8-inch pan. Cool and cut into squares.

Yields: 30 to 36 squares.

❄

FAVORITE PRALINES

————— · · · · · —————

This favorite treat is now easy and time saving
with the microwave oven.

½ cup sugar
1 cup brown sugar
   (dark brown works
   well)
¼ teaspoon salt

¾ cup milk or light cream
   or evaporated milk
1¼ cups whole pecan
   halves
1 tablespoon butter
½ teaspoon vanilla

1. Combine sugars, salt, and milk in a 2-quart bowl, mixing well. Microwave for 9 to 12 minutes at MEDIUM HIGH (70%) until mixture forms a soft ball (232°F.) when a small amount is dropped into a small dish of cold water, stirring twice. Stir in pecans and microwave for 1 minute at HIGH (100%).

2. Stir in butter and vanilla. Beat the mixture slightly until glossy (1 minute). Drop by tablespoonfuls onto waxed paper. Let stand until firm. Store wrapped individually in plastic wrap or in single layers in an airtight container.

Yields: 25 2-inch pralines.

————— · ❄ · —————

Every great work accomplished by man was called impossible at first.

I remember a friend calling me near Christmas a few years ago. She had microwaved her almond bark for 8 minutes at HIGH (100%) and wanted to know if she could fix the ruined crumbly chocolate. Unfortunately, she could not.

When using a full-size, 600- or 700-watt microwave oven, do not microwave chocolate chips or almond bark at HIGH (100%), and do not expect it to look melted after 2 to 3 minutes. Chocolate chips or almond bark will look soft, puffy, and shiny when melted. It will look melted after stirring.

PEANUT CLUSTERS
OR CHOCOLATE HAYSTACKS

——— · · · · · ———

2 cups chocolate chips   16 ounces peanuts
16 ounces white almond
  bark

1. Microwave chocolate chips and almond bark for 2 minutes at MEDIUM HIGH (70%). Stir. Microwave again for 1 minute at MEDIUM HIGH (70%). Stir. Continue to microwave in 30-second intervals and stir until mixture is melted.
2. Stir in peanuts. Drop by teaspoonfuls onto waxed paper or into small paper cups.

Yields: 3 to 4 dozen candies.

——— · ❄ · ———

Compacts: Follow this same recipe, microwaving at HIGH (100%) instead of MEDIUM HIGH (70%).

Variation: For Chocolate Haystacks, omit almond bark and substitute 2 cans (3 ounces each) chow mein noodles for peanuts. Proceed as directed above.

CANDIED PRETZELS

———— · · · · · ————

16 ounces almond bark
2 tablespoons vegetable
  oil

2 dozen pretzels
powdered sugar or
  colored sugars

1. Microwave almond bark and oil in a 2-quart casserole for 3 to 4 minutes at MEDIUM HIGH (70%) until it can be stirred smooth (melted).

2. Dip pretzels in coating using tongs. Roll in powdered sugar. Place on waxed paper and chill until firm.

Yields: 24 pretzels.

———— · ❋ · ————

Troubles are often the tools by which God fashions us for better things.

CAKES

. . . . .

- **Cakes do not brown** in a microwave oven, so take advantage of this and **use colored cake mixes or those with fruit or colored chips. Frosting is easier** without the brown crumbs, anyway!

- Use any microwave-safe cake dish. Rounded dishes work best, especially those with a center tube because they produce the most even cooking results. **When possible use a microwave bundt or tube pan,** which helps the microwaves penetrate and bake the center thoroughly.

- A tube-pan effect may be produced by inserting a drinking glass open-ended into the center of a microwave-safe mixing bowl. Mix, insert the glass, and bake in the same dish!

- **Always grease a cake dish with oil or spray shortening and then dust with sugar. DO NOT USE FLOUR** for dusting. The cake will stick to the dish if you do.

- If a layer cake is to be unmolded, line the bottom of the baking dish with waxed paper for easy removal.

- Fill cake dishes only ⅔ full, as microwaved cakes rise more than conventionally baked ones. (Use leftover batter for cupcakes and cones.)

- A cake will test done when a toothpick inserted near the center comes out clean. A few moist spots may appear on top of a cake after cooking. They will evaporate. If the center starts to sink, microwave the cake longer.

- Place the cake dish on an inverted saucer or pie plate while microwaving if you find that the bottom of your cakes do not get done. (More microwaves will reach the bottom of your cake.)

- **Always shield corners of square dishes with foil to prevent hardened corners.** (See shielding section on pages 9 and 10.)

- Decrease water/liquids by 1 tablespoon per cup of water or liquid in most recipes when converting from a conventional to a microwave recipe.

CAKE MICROWAVING CHART

CAKE DISH SIZE	1ST TIME/POWER	2ND TIME/POWER	STANDING TIME
PUDDING IN THE MIX CAKE MIXES:			
Bundt	10 minutes/Defrost (30%)	5–7 minutes/High (100%)	10 minutes
Single layer–9"	6 minutes/Defrost (30%)	3–4 minutes/High (100%)	10 minutes
Full-size–12"x8"	10 minutes/Defrost (30%)	4–6 minutes/High (100%)	10 minutes
HOMEMADE & BOX CAKE MIXES:			
Ring or bundt	9–10 minutes/Medium High (70%)	4–5 minutes/High (100%)	10–15 minutes
For compacts	11–15 minutes/High (100%)		10–15 minutes
Ring or bundt with delicate ingredients (fruit, sour cream, etc.)	12 minutes/Medium (50%)	3–7 minutes/High (100%)	15 minutes
Single layer or small ring–9" square or 8" square or 10"x6"	5 minutes/Medium High (70%)	1¼–2 minutes/High (100%)	5 minutes
With delicate ingredients	6 minutes/Medium (50%)	4–6 minutes/High (100%)	5 minutes
For compacts	7–9 minutes/High (100%)		5 minutes
Full size–12"x8"	9 minutes/Medium (50%)	3–7 minutes/High (100%)	5 minutes
CUPCAKES:			
1	25–30 seconds/High (100%)		1 minute
2	45–75 seconds/High (100%)		1 minute
4	1½–2 minutes/High (100%)		1 minute
6	2–3 minutes/High (100%)		1 minute
BARS–BROWNIES:	5½–7 minutes/High (100%)		10 minutes
With delicate ingredients	7 minutes/Medium (50%)	3–4 minutes/High (100%)	10 minutes

FRESH APPLE COFFEE CAKE

——— · · · · · ———

· CAKE ·

¼ cup butter or margarine
¾ cup brown sugar
2 eggs
1 teaspoon vanilla
½ cup flour
½ teaspoon soda
dash of salt

½ teaspoon cinnamon
1 cup oats
1 cup chopped apple
¼ cup water
1 recipe Basic
     Buttercream Frosting
     (page 104)

· TOPPING ·

¼ cup sugar
1 teaspoon cinnamon

¼ cup chopped nuts

1. Microwave butter in a 2-quart bowl for 25 seconds at HIGH (100%). Beat in sugar, eggs, and vanilla until fluffy.

2. Combine flour, soda, salt, cinnamon, and oats. Stir into egg mixture.

3. Stir in apple and water.

4. Pour batter into a 9-inch round dish or ring pan. Combine topping ingredients and sprinkle over batter.

*5. Microwave for 7 minutes at MEDIUM (50%), and microwave again for 3 to 4½ minutes at HIGH (100%). Let stand 5 minutes.

6. Serve warm, drizzled with heated buttercream frosting.

Yields: one 9-inch cake.

——— · ❄ · ———

Compacts: Microwave for 9 to 10 minutes at HIGH (100%) instead of step #5.

· ·
*Rotate dish once if necessary for even cooking.

This is a fast favorite of mine that I often make in the fall, but since the recipe uses canned applesauce it can be made anytime. Drizzled with Vanilla Frosting, this cake is sure to be your favorite, too.

The pan is placed on an inverted saucer in the microwave oven so the microwaves will bounce off the floor of the oven and cook the bottom side evenly.

APPLESAUCE SWIRL CAKE

· · · · ·

⅓ cup chopped nuts
¼ cup brown sugar
2 teaspoons cinnamon
1 package yellow cake mix (with pudding)
3 eggs

1½ cups applesauce (12-ounce jar)
⅓ cup oil
Powdered sugar or 1 recipe Vanilla Frosting (page 104)

1. Grease and sugar a microwave bundt pan. Sprinkle with nuts.

2. Combine brown sugar and cinnamon. Set aside.

3. Combine cake mix, eggs, applesauce, and oil. Beat 2 minutes.

4. Pour ½ of the batter in the pan. Sprinkle with sugar mixture. Cover with remaining batter. Place on an inverted saucer in the microwave.

*5. Microwave for 12 minutes at MEDIUM (50%), and again for 5 to 6 minutes at HIGH (100%).

6. Let stand 15 minutes. Invert. Sprinkle with powdered sugar or drizzle with Vanilla Frosting (microwaved for 20 seconds).

Yields: 1 bundt cake.

❄

Compacts: Microwave for 12 to 14 minutes at HIGH (100%) instead of step #5.

* Rotate pan twice if necessary for even cooking.

FAVORITE UPSIDE-DOWN CAKE

—— · · · · · ——

Fresh peach or canned pineapple is especially yummy!

· TOPPING ·

1 cup sliced fruit (fresh or canned), well drained	1 cup brown sugar
	2 tablespoons butter

· CAKE ·

1 cup sugar	2½ teaspoons baking
⅓ cup butter	powder
1⅓ cups flour	⅓ cup lemonade concen-
2 tablespoons cornstarch	trate, undiluted, or
dash of salt	milk
	2 eggs

1. **For fresh fruit:** Cook fruit in a covered glass dish for 3 to 5 minutes at HIGH (100%). Drain well. (Start with 3 peaches or apples, etc.) **For canned fruit:** Just drain well. (Use an 8-ounce can of crushed pineapple or 1 cup any other fruit.)

2. Combine all ingredients for topping in a greased microwave ring pan. Microwave 4 to 5 minutes at HIGH (100%) until boiling and thickened. Cool completely.

3. Combine all ingredients for cake, using a food processor, blender, or mixer. Beat well.

4. Spoon batter over cooled topping in ring pan.

5. Microwave for 12 minutes at MEDIUM (50%). Rotate dish, if necessary, for even cooking. Microwave again for 1 to 4 minutes at HIGH (100%). Top will look moist.

6. Let stand 5 minutes. Invert.

Yields: 1 ring cake (8 servings).

—— · ❄ · ——

Compacts: Microwave 12 to 15 minutes at HIGH (100%).

Cool the topping after cooking to prevent it from baking into the cake.

Orange juice concentrate may be used to replace the lemonade concentrate, if desired.

BLACK FOREST CAKE
WITH CHERRY GLAZE

———— · · · · · ————

Sounds difficult to make, but it's a snap!

· CAKE ·

19-ounce package chocolate cake mix
2 large eggs
⅓ cup water

⅓ cup oil
1 teaspoon vanilla or almond flavoring
21-ounce can cherry pie filling

· GLAZE ·

1 tablespoon margarine
1 cup powdered sugar

4 tablespoons water (plus reserved syrup)
½ teaspoon cherry flavoring

1. Using a food processor or mixer, combine all cake ingredients, except the pie filling. Beat well.

2. Remove 1 tablespoon of the syrup from the pie filling for the glaze.

3. Stir the remaining pie filling into the cake batter.

4. Pour into a greased and sugared microwave bundt pan. Place on an inverted saucer.

* 5. Microwave for 11 minutes at DEFROST (30%) and again for 6 to 7 minutes at HIGH (100%).

6. Let stand 5 minutes. Invert. Cool.

7. **Glaze:** In a 1-quart bowl, microwave margarine for 25 seconds at HIGH (100%) until melted. Stir in reserved syrup, water, and flavoring. Microwave for 1 minute at HIGH (100%). Beat in powdered sugar. Microwave 30 seconds at HIGH (100%). Pour over cake.

Yields: 1 bundt cake (12 servings).

———— · ❊ · ————

Compacts: Microwave cake for 12 to 14 minutes at HIGH (100%) instead of step #5.

· ·
* Rotate cake twice while microwaving, if necessary, for even cooking.

MICROWAVE CHOCOLATE CRAZY CAKE

· · · · ·

No cleanup—mix and bake in the same dish.
A delicious single-layer chocolate cake.

1½ cups flour	1 tablespoon vinegar
1 cup sugar	⅓ cup vegetable oil
1 teaspoon soda	¾ cup plus 2 tablespoons
½ teaspoon salt	cold water
3 tablespoons cocoa	1 recipe Chocolate
1 teaspoon vanilla	Chipper Frosting
	(page 103)

1. Sift dry ingredients into a 9-inch square or round microwave-safe pan that has been greased and sugared. Make 3 wells in the dry ingredients.

2. Place vanilla, vinegar, and oil in each well, distributing evenly.

3. Pour water over all and blend thoroughly with a fork, but do not beat.

* 4. Microwave for 7 minutes at MEDIUM (50%) and for 2½ to 3½ minutes at HIGH (100%). Shield corners with foil if using a square pan. Cool.

5. Frost with Chocolate Chipper Frosting.

Yields: one 9-inch cake.

──────── · ❄ · ────────

Compacts: Microwave one 9-inch pan for 9 to 10 minutes at HIGH (100%) instead of step #4.

Variation: Double the recipe and make a 2-layer cake. Double the frosting, too. Pour batter into two 9-inch round layer cake pans or into one 8x12-inch pan. Microwave 9-inch pans individually as directed above. Microwave 8x12-inch pan for 10 minutes at MEDIUM (50%) and 3 to 4 minutes at HIGH (100%) with corners shielded.

· ·
* Rotate pan once, if necessary, for even cooking.

This is a similar recipe to the one-bowl recipe we've all made for years in a conventional oven. It works well in the microwave, too.

This cake can be convection-microwaved for traditional browning: Choose the convection microwave setting that corresponds to your oven.

One layer = 20 minutes at Convection-Microwave (Low-Mix) Bake 350°F. OR Combination #2 or Code #2.

Two layers = 25 minutes at Convection-Microwave (Low-Mix) Bake 350°F. OR Combination #2 OR Code #2.

HAWAIIAN PINEAPPLE CAKE

———— · · · · · ————

*It's delicious and easy—a nice small cake for a brunch
or coffee.*

· CAKE ·

1 cup flour	½ teaspoon baking soda
1 tablespoon cornstarch	1 egg
⅔ cup sugar	8-ounce can crushed
½ teaspoon salt	pineapple

· TOPPING ·

⅓ cup brown sugar	⅓ cup chopped nuts or
	almonds

· GLAZE ·

⅓ cup milk	½ cup sugar
5 tablespoons butter	1 teaspoon vanilla

1. Combine all cake ingredients thoroughly. Pour into a greased and sugared 8- or 9-inch round pan. (If you use a square pan, shield corners with foil.)

2. Combine topping ingredients. Sprinkle over the cake batter.

*3. Cover with plastic wrap. Microwave for 6 minutes at MEDIUM (50%). Microwave again for 3 to 4 minutes at HIGH (100%).

4. In a 1-cup glass measure, combine glaze ingredients. Microwave for 2 to 3 minutes at HIGH (100%) until boiling. Pour over warm cake. Cool.

Yields: one 8- or 9-inch cake.

———— · ❄ · ————

· ·
*Rotate pan once, if necessary, for even cooking.

HOT FUDGE SUNDAE CAKE

. . . . .

A dessert the kids like to make. It creates its own fudge sauce on the bottom as a cake layer forms on the top.

· CAKE ·

1 cup flour
⅔ cup sugar
2 tablespoons cocoa
2 teaspoons baking
  powder
dash of salt
½ cup milk

2 tablespoons vegetable
  oil
1 teaspoon vanilla
1 cup miniature marsh-
  mallows
½ cup chopped nuts

· TOPPING ·

1 cup brown sugar,
  packed

¼ cup cocoa
½ cup hot water

1. Combine all the dry ingredients for the cake in a 9-inch round microwave pan with tall sides. Stir in milk, oil, and vanilla until smooth. Stir in marshmallows and nuts.

2. Sprinkle with the brown sugar and cocoa for the topping.

3. Microwave the hot water in a 2-cup measure for 2 to 3 minutes at HIGH (100%) or until boiling. Pour water over batter—do not stir. Cover with a large paper towel.

*4. Microwave cake for 8½ to 9½ minutes at HIGH (100%) until no longer doughy.

5. Let stand 5 minutes. Spoon cake and sauce into serving dishes.

Yields: one 9-inch cake.

———— · ❄ · ————

Compacts: Microwave cake for 10 to 11 minutes in step #4.

. . . .
*Rotate cake twice during cooking, if necessary, for even cooking.

Use a pan with 2½-inch sides. A pie plate will not work because the batter will spill over the sides while cooking.

Place pan on an inverted saucer in the microwave oven so the microwaves will bounce off the floor of the oven and cook the bottom side.

Using the MEDIUM (50%) power setting first is very important here because it allows the cake time to rise slowly. The HIGH (100%) setting then quickly finishes cooking it.

To ensure that the bottom of the cake will cook evenly, place the pan on an inverted saucer in the microwave oven so the microwaves will bounce off the floor of the oven and cook the bottom side.

Mix up this easy recipe and have it on hand.

3 cups flour	1 teaspoon salt
3 tablespoons cornstarch	½ cup powdered milk
2⅔ cups sugar	1 cup plus 1 tablespoon
5 teaspoons baking	shortening
powder	

1. Using a food processor or mixer, combine all the dry ingredients.

2. Add the shortening and process or mix until mixture is thoroughly blended and crumbly. Put in a large airtight container and store in a cool dry place. (This mix keeps for 10 to 12 weeks.)

Yields: 6 cups.

· ❉ ·

To use any of the following in cake recipes: Beat amount of mix listed with liquid ingredients for 2 minutes; pour into a greased and sugared small microwave ring pan or 8-inch round pan for 1-layer cakes, or a microwave bundt pan or 8x12-inch glass pan for the family-sized or bundt cakes. For square or rectangular pans: Always shield the corners with foil until the last 2 to 3 minutes of the microwaving time. (See shielding section on pages 9 and 10.) Microwave at time and power listed. Rotate once or twice, if necessary, for even cooking.

VARIATIONS

· YELLOW CAKE (1-LAYER) ·

2 cups microwave cake
  mix
1 egg
½ cup water

1 teaspoon vanilla,
  almond, lemon, or
  orange extract

Microwave for 5 minutes at MEDIUM (50%). Microwave again for 3 to 5 minutes at HIGH (100%). Cool.

· WHITE CAKE (1 LAYER) ·

2 cups microwave cake
  mix
2 egg whites

⅓ cup water
1 teaspoon vanilla

Microwave for 5 minutes at MEDIUM (50%). Microwave again for 3 to 5 minutes at HIGH (100%). Cool.

· CHOCOLATE CAKE (1-LAYER) ·

2 cups microwave cake
  mix
1 egg
½ cup water

⅓ cup cocoa
2 tablespoons milk
2 tablespoons butter

Microwave for 5 minutes at MEDIUM (50%). Microwave again for 4 to 5½ minutes at HIGH (100%). Cool.

· DATE CAKE (1 LAYER) ·

2 cups microwave cake
  mix
1 egg
½ teaspoon vanilla
½ teaspoon cinnamon
½ cup very hot water
  (pour over dates first
  for 10 minutes to
  soften)

½ cup dates
⅓ cup brown sugar
⅓ cup nuts
⅓ cup chocolate chips

Beat mix, egg, vanilla, and cinnamon. Add dates and water; beat. Sprinkle with brown sugar, nuts, and chocolate chips. Microwave for 5 minutes at MEDIUM (50%) and again for 4 to 6 minutes at HIGH (100%). Cool.

· POPPY SEED CAKE (1 LAYER) ·

2 cups microwave cake mix	½ cup water
	1 egg
2 teaspoons grated orange or lemon peel	3 tablespoons poppy seed

Microwave for 5 minutes at MEDIUM (50%). Microwave again for 3 to 5 minutes at HIGH (100%). Cool. Drizzle with lemon or orange glaze.

· CHERRY DESSERT CAKE ·

1 can cherry pie filling	½ cup margarine
2 cups cake mix	½ cup sliced almonds or nuts

Layer in order: cherry pie filling, cake mix, margarine, and almonds or nuts. Do not mix together. Microwave for 5 minutes at MEDIUM (50%). Microwave again for 4 to 6 minutes at HIGH (100%). Cool.

· ORANGE CAKE ·

Follow directions for Yellow Cake. Substitute ⅓ cup frozen orange juice concentrate for the water. Use orange extract. Glaze.

· LEMON CAKE ·

Follow directions for Yellow Cake. Substitute ⅓ cup frozen lemonade concentrate for the water. Use lemon extract. Glaze.

· BUNDT CAKE ·

Double any cake recipe (use 4 cups mix). Microwave for 9 minutes at MEDIUM (50%). Microwave again for 4 to 5 minutes at HIGH (100%). Let stand 10 minutes.

· FAMILY-SIZE CAKE ·

Use an 8x12-inch pan. Shield corners with foil. Follow directions for bundt cake.

Compacts: Microwave 1-layer cake for 6 to 7 minutes at HIGH (100%). Microwave bundt or family cake for 11 to 13 minutes at HIGH (100%).

SELF-FROSTED GERMAN CHOCOLATE CAKE
(FROM A BOX MIX)

· · · · ·

¼ cup butter
1 9.9-ounce package
   coconut pecan frosting
   mix
⅓ cup milk
3 eggs

18-ounce package
   (pudding in the mix)
   German chocolate cake
   mix
¼ cup oil
1¼ cups water

1. In a microwave bundt pan, melt butter by microwaving for 10 to 30 seconds at HIGH (100%). Stir in frosting mix and milk. Microwave for 1 minute at HIGH (100%). Spread evenly in the pan.

2. Using a mixer, beat the remaining ingredients for 2 minutes.

3. Pour over frosting in bundt pan. Place on an inverted saucer in the microwave.

*4. Microwave for 11 minutes at DEFROST (30%) and again for 6 to 7 minutes at HIGH (100%).

5. Let stand in pan 5 to 10 minutes, but not longer. Invert and spread cake with any remaining topping in dish.

Yields: 1 frosted bundt cake.

——— · ❄ · ———

Compacts: Microwave for 12 to 15 minutes at HIGH (100%) instead of step #4.

Variation: Coconut-pecan frosting from scratch—omit frosting mix, butter, and milk in step #1. Substitute "TOPPING" ingredients and follow step #2 only on page 80. Proceed as directed above beginning with step #3.

· ·

*Rotate pan, if necessary, twice for even cooking.

If you don't have a frosting mix on hand, you can make the cake from the mix and use the scratch frosting variations (see the Variation for details).

Name brand cake mixes usually work better than generic brands. I prefer Pillsbury or Betty Crocker.

½ cup margarine (1 stick)
1 cup sugar
½ teaspoon grated orange
  peel
2 eggs
¼ cup water
1½ teaspoons baking soda
1½ teaspoons baking
  powder
2 cups flour

½ teaspoon salt
¼ teaspoon nutmeg
1 teaspoon cinnamon
1 cup coarsely chopped
  raisins
2 cups finely grated
  carrots
1 recipe Cream Cheese
  Frosting (page 105)

1. Using a food processor or mixer, cream margarine, sugar, and orange peel. Add eggs and water. Beat.

2. Combine dry ingredients. Beat into creamed mixture.

3. Stir in raisins and carrots.

4. **For an 8x12-inch cake:** Pour into a greased and sugared baking dish. Shield corners with foil. Microwave for 12 minutes at MEDIUM (50%). Microwave again for 4 to 6 minutes at HIGH (100%). Let stand 5 minutes. **For a bundt or ring cake:** Pour into a greased and sugared tube pan. Microwave for 10 minutes at MEDIUM HIGH (70%). Microwave again for 4 to 5 minutes at HIGH (100%). Let stand 5 minutes. Invert.

5. Frost with Cream Cheese Frosting.

Yields: one 8x12-inch or bundt cake.

. ❄ .

RHUBARB CAKE

————— · · · · · —————

4 cups diced rhubarb
1 cup sugar
1 package strawberry Jello
2 cups miniature
   marshmallows

18-ounce package white
   or yellow cake mix plus
   oil, eggs, and water as
   per package directions

1. Grease and sugar an 8x12-inch microwave pan. Place diced rhubarb in pan. Sprinkle with sugar, Jello, and marshmallows. Mix well.

2. Prepare cake mix according to package directions.

3. Pour cake batter over all.

*4. Shield corners with foil. Microwave for 10 minutes at MEDIUM (50%) and microwave again for 3 to 6 minutes at HIGH (100%).

5. Cool 30 minutes. Serve with whipped topping.

Yields: one 8x12-inch cake.

————— · ❄ · —————

Compacts: Microwave for 12 to 14 minutes at HIGH (100%) instead of Step #4 with corners shielded.

TIPS
· · · · ·

This is a quick way to use fresh or frozen rhubarb. I often freeze garden rhubarb in freezer bags of 4 cups each. Right before using it, I microwave the frozen rhubarb in the bag for 2½ to 3 minutes at HIGH (100%). Then I use the rhubarb immediately before it is completely thawed.

· ·

*Rotate pan twice during microwaving, if necessary, for even cooking.

Red raspberry preserves look more attractive as a topping than black raspberry preserves. Try substituting orange marmalade for the preserves. Just make sure that you use name-brand marmalade or preserves as thinner preserves do not set up well in the frosting.

You can use up to twice as much coconut if you like. For people who do not like coconut—the ⅓ cup of coconut used in this recipe can hardly be tasted (but it does help hold the frosting together).

SELF-FROSTED RASPBERRY AND LEMON CAKE

———— · · · · · ————

Or try any flavored cake mix with pudding and any preserves for variety.

3 tablespoons margarine
  or butter
⅔ cup raspberry preserves
  (or any flavor)
⅓ cup coconut
1 cup water OR as package
  directs

18-ounce package lemon
  cake mix with pudding
  (or any flavor)
3 eggs
⅓ cup oil OR as package
  directs

1. Grease and sugar a microwave bundt or ring pan.
2. Melt margarine in the pan by microwaving for 30 to 40 seconds at HIGH (100%). Mix preserves and coconut with melted margarine, spreading evenly.
3. Mix cake mix as directed on the package, using the remaining ingredients.
4. Pour batter over the preserves in the bundt pan. Place on an inverted saucer in the microwave.
5. Microwave for 11 minutes at DEFROST (30%) and again for 5 to 6 minutes at HIGH (100%) or until no longer doughy, rotating twice, if necessary, for even cooking.
6. Let stand 5 to 10 minutes and invert. Cool completely.

Yields: 1 bundt cake (12 servings).

———— · ❄ · ————

Compacts: Microwave 12 to 15 minutes at HIGH (100%).

SELF-FROSTED GERMAN CHOCOLATE CAKE

(FROM SCRATCH)

· · · · ·

· CAKE ·

4-ounce bar German
  chocolate
1 cup sugar
6 tablespoons margarine
½ teaspoon salt
½ teaspoon baking
  powder

½ teaspoon baking soda
¾ cup sour milk or buttermilk
4 teaspoons cornstarch
1¼ cups flour
2 eggs
1 teaspoon vanilla

· TOPPING ·

⅓ cup margarine
⅔ cup brown sugar
⅔ cup chopped pecans or
  nuts

⅔ cup coconut
¼ cup evaporated milk or
  cream

1. For cake: Microwave chocolate in a small dish for 1 to 2 minutes at MEDIUM HIGH (70%) until melted. Using a food processor or mixer, cream melted chocolate, sugar, margarine, salt, baking powder, and soda. Beat in sour milk, cornstarch, and flour. Beat in eggs and vanilla. Set aside.

2. For topping: Microwave margarine and brown sugar in a microwave ring or bundt pan for 1 to 2 minutes at HIGH (100%) until bubbly. Stir and spread evenly. Sprinkle with pecans and coconut. Pour milk over coconut. Microwave again for 1 to 1½ minutes at HIGH (100%) until bubbly. Stir and spread evenly.

3. Pour cake batter over hot topping. Place on an inverted saucer in the microwave.

4. Microwave for 12 minutes at MEDIUM (50%). Rotate dish, if necessary, for even cooking. Microwave again for 4 to 5 minutes at HIGH (100%).

5. Let stand 5 minutes. Invert and spread any remaining topping in dish on cake.

Yields: 1 ring or bundt cake.

———— · ❄ · ————

Compacts: Microwave for 12 to 15 minutes at HIGH (100%). Rotate pan, if necessary, twice for even cooking.

Variation: Use a box frosting mix for greater ease. Instead of making this topping in step #2, mix a Betty Crocker coconut pecan frosting mix with ⅓ cup milk and ¼ cup butter. Microwave for 1 to 2 minutes at HIGH (100%) until bubbly. Continue with step #3.

. . . .

Character is nurtured midst the tempests of the world.

T I P S
· · · · ·

Most cakes will not miss a few spoonfuls of batter. Children love to watch batter rise in such a short time. Top with a scoop of ice cream for ice cream and cake in a cone.

INDIVIDUAL ICE CREAM CONE CAKES

———— · · · · · ————

A nice treat from leftover cake batter.

flat-bottomed ice cream
   cones
cake batter—your favorite
   (2 tablespoons per cone)

frosting
candied sprinkles for
   decoration

1. Spoon 2 tablespoons cake batter into each cone.
2. Microwave for 15 to 20 seconds per cone at HIGH (100%). Let stand 1 to 2 minutes and moist spots will disappear. (Microwave only 1 cone at a time because some cones will melt with prolonged cooking.)
3. Frost and decorate with sprinkles as you like.

COOKIES, BARS, AND FROSTINGS

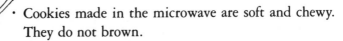

- Cookies made in the microwave are soft and chewy. They do not brown.

- **Baked cookies may be refreshed to that "just-baked taste"** by microwaving 3 to 4 cookies for 15 seconds at HIGH (100%).

- Big batches do not save time using the microwave, so use your conventional oven. **Small batches do save time and energy when baked in the microwave oven.**

- Bar cookies work best when a bar recipe adjusted especially for the microwave oven is followed.

- **Use waxed paper for the cookie sheet**—placed on a microwave tray, a piece of cardboard, or a large paper plate.

- Allow space between cookies because they spread during cooking.

- **Microwave no more than twelve cookies at one time**—actually six to nine cookies bake the best at once.

- **Cookies will burn in the middle if overbaked.**

- **For bars: Follow the same preparation suggestions as for cakes** (see pages 63 and 64), especially for greasing and sugaring the pan, as well as testing doneness and SHIELDING. (See shielding section on pages 9 and 10.)

COOKIES AND BARS

· ❄ ·

COOKIE BAKING CHART

	TIME/POWER LEVEL	ALL COOKIES SHOULD STAND 2 MINUTES
NUMBER OF COOKIES		
4	2½–3½ minutes at MEDIUM (50%)	
6	3–4 minutes at MEDIUM (100%)	
9	4–5 minutes at MEDIUM (50%)	
12	5–6 minutes at MEDIUM (50%)	
COMPACTS 6–9 cookies	2–3 minutes at HIGH (100%)	
BARS AND BROWNIES 8 inch-square pan with sensitive ingredients	5½–7 minutes at HIGH (100%) 7 minutes at MEDIUM (50%) plus 3–4 minutes at HIGH (100%)	
12x8-inch pan	10 minutes at MEDIUM (50%) plus 2–4 minutes at HIGH	
COMPACTS 8 inch-square pan	7–7½ minutes at HIGH (100%)	

APRICOT BARS

—— · · · · · ——

Nice to take to a special party!

1½ cups flour
1 teaspoon baking powder
¼ teaspoon salt
1½ cups rolled oats
   (quick)

1 cup brown sugar
⅔ cup butter or margarine
¾ cup apricot preserves or
   jam

1. Mix flour, baking powder, and salt thoroughly. Stir in oats and sugar. Microwave butter in an 8-inch square microwave pan at HIGH (100%) for 20 seconds or until soft. Stir in dry ingredients until crumbly. Remove half of the crumbly mixture for topping. Press remainder into the pan.

*2. Microwave for 4 to 5 minutes at MEDIUM HIGH (70%).

3. Spread with jam. Top with remaining crumbly mixture.

*4. Microwave for 3 to 4 minutes on MEDIUM HIGH (70%) with corners shielded with foil. Cool and cut into bars.

Yields: 16 bars.

—— · ❄ · ——

· ·
* Rotate pan once each microwaving time, if necessary, for even cooking.

When I need a fast dessert, I always make these bars and serve them with a scoop of ice cream.

These bars firm up when cooled.

EASY CHERRY BARS
(OR TRY BLUEBERRY BARS)
———— · · · · · ————

1 can cherry pie filling (or blueberry, etc.)
9 ounces Jiffy cake mix

3 tablespoons margarine, sliced
½ cup brown sugar
½ cup chopped nuts

1. Grease and sugar an 8x8-inch microwave-safe pan. Layer all ingredients in the pan in order given.
2. Shield corners with foil.
* 3. Microwave for 10 minutes at HIGH (100%).
4. Let stand until cooled.

Yields: 16 to 24 bars.

———— · ❄ · ————

Compacts: Microwave for 12 minutes at HIGH (100%) in step #3.

· ·
* Rotate dish once, if necessary, for even cooking.

FUDGE BROWNIES
(WITH VARIATIONS)

———— · · · · · ————

Delicious and ready to eat in 6 minutes.

½ cup butter or margarine
⅓ cup cocoa
1 cup sugar
2 eggs
1 teaspoon vanilla
¼ teaspoon salt

½ teaspoon baking
   powder
¾ cup flour
½ cup chopped nuts
   (optional)
1 recipe Chocolate
   Chipper Frosting (page
   103), optional

1. Microwave butter and cocoa in a 2-quart bowl for 1 minute at HIGH (100%). Stir in sugar and mix thoroughly.

2. Blend in eggs and vanilla.

3. Combine remaining dry ingredients and add to cocoa batter. Stir until well blended. Add nuts.

4. Spread into a greased and sugared 8-inch square microwave-safe pan. Shield corners with foil.

*5. Microwave for 5½ to 6 minutes at HIGH (100%) until top is no longer wet. (Remove foil for the last 2 minutes of cooking time.) Let stand 5 minutes.

6. Frost if desired with Chocolate Chipper Frosting.

Yields: 16 bars.

———— · · ————

──

*Rotate pan twice, if necessary, for even cooking.

If your microwave oven is an older model that does not allow for the use of foil, use a round pan. If you use a square pan without the foil shielding, the corners will be crunchy and slightly overcooked. One woman at one of my microwave classes said that her children love the crunchy corners!

See shielding section on pages 9 and 10 for tips on shielding.

VARIATIONS

Rocky Road Brownies: After microwaving in step #5, sprinkle hot bars with 1 cup miniature marshmallows. Let stand, then drizzle with Chocolate Chipper Frosting.

Peanut Butter Brownies: Decrease butter by 2 tablespoons and add ¼ cup peanut butter in step #1. Add 1 tablespoon peanut butter to the butter in the Chocolate Chipper Frosting recipe before frosting.

Mississippi Mud Cake: Add ½ cup pecans instead of nuts. Add ⅔ cup coconut. Microwave as directed. While still hot, spread with 4 ounces marshmallow creme or 1½ cups miniature marshmallows, spreading after they have melted. Frost with Chocolate Buttercream Frosting (see page 104).

. . . .

Cheerfulness and contentment are great beautifiers, and are famous preservers of youthful looks.

BLONDE BROWNIES
(WITH VARIATIONS)

—————— · · · · · ——————

¾ cup brown sugar,
  packed
1 stick margarine (½ cup)
2 eggs
1 teaspoon vanilla
¼ teaspoon baking
  powder

¾ cup flour
dash of salt
¼ cup chopped nuts
½ cup plus ¼ cup semi-
  sweet chocolate chips
Powdered sugar or
  Butterscotch Frosting
  (page 104)

TIPS
· · · · ·

If you increase the baking powder in the Blonde Brownie recipe, the brownies will rise more and resemble a cake.

See shielding section on pages 9 and 10 for tips on shielding.

1. Microwave brown sugar and margarine in a 2-quart microwave bowl for 1 minute at HIGH (100%).

2. Blend in eggs and vanilla.

3. Combine remaining dry ingredients and add to brown sugar batter. Stir until well blended. Add nuts and ½ cup chocolate chips.

4. Spread into a greased and sugared 8-inch square microwave-safe pan. Shield corners with foil.

* 5. Microwave for 4 minutes at HIGH (100%). Remove foil. Sprinkle with ¼ cup chocolate chips. Microwave again for 1½ to 2 minutes at HIGH (100%). Let stand 30 minutes. Sprinkle with powdered sugar or frost with Butterscotch Frosting.

Yields: 16 bars.

—————— · ❄ · ——————

· ·
* Rotate pan twice, if necessary, for even cooking.

VARIATIONS

Chocolate Chip Bars: Add ⅓ cup flour and substitute ½ teaspoon soda for the ¼ teaspoon baking powder. Follow the recipe as given.

Chocolate Chip Cake: Follow Blonde Brownies recipe, but increase the baking powder to 1 teaspoon.

Raisins are the secret ingredient for this cakelike
treat.

See shielding section on
pages 9 and 10 for instructions on shielding.

If you have a convection
microwave oven, use the
convection microwave
variation. Three convec-
tion microwave settings
are suggested. Choose the
one that corresponds to
the power setting on your
convection microwave.

AUNT DADE'S DELICIOUS CAKE
BROWNIES

———— . . . . . ————

2 sticks margarine (1 cup)	3 eggs
⅓ cup cocoa	1½ cups flour
1¾ cups sugar	1 cup raisins
2 teaspoons vanilla	powdered sugar for garnish

1. Place margarine and cocoa in an 8x12-inch microwave-safe dish. Microwave for 40 to 50 seconds at MEDIUM HIGH (70%) until margarine is melted. Stir well.

2. Mix in sugar and vanilla; then eggs; then flour. Stir in raisins. Shield corners with foil. Place on an inverted saucer in the microwave.

3. Microwave for 8 minutes at MEDIUM (50%).

4. Remove foil. Microwave again for 2 to 4 minutes at HIGH (100%) to finish baking. Cool.

5. Dust with powdered sugar.

Yields: 24 bars.

———— · ❄ · ————

Compacts: Instead of steps #3 and #4, shield corners with foil and microwave for 8 to 9 minutes at HIGH (100%).

For convection microwave: Instead of steps #3 and #4, Convection Microwave Low-Mix Bake at 350°F. for 20 to 22 minutes OR Combination #2 OR Code #2 for 20 to 22 minutes.

. . . .

Anyone can carry his burden, however hard, until nightfall. Anyone can do his work, however hard, for one day.

CHEWY OATMEAL BARS

— · · · · · —

Nutritious and delicious.

1 stick margarine (½ cup)	2 cups oats (quick)
½ cup brown sugar, packed	1 cup chocolate chips
½ cup honey	½ cup peanut butter (chunky or creamy)

1. Microwave margarine, brown sugar, and honey for 1 minute at HIGH (100%) in an 8-inch microwave dish. Stir well and then stir in oats. Spread evenly and press into dish.

2. Microwave for 5 to 6 minutes at MEDIUM HIGH (70%) until bubbly. Cool.

3. Microwave chocolate chips and peanut butter in a 2-cup measure for 2 minutes at HIGH (100%). Stir until smooth. Spread on top of oatmeal base. Refrigerate and cut into squares when firm.

Yields: 16 bars.

——— · ❄ · ———

Compacts: Microwave for 4 to 5 minutes at HIGH (100%) in step #2.

Too many folks go through life running from something that isn't after them.

DATE BARS

· · · · ·

· FILLING ·

1½ cups chopped dates　　¼ cup sugar

　　　　　　　　　　　　½ cup water

· BASE ·

½ cup butter or　　　　1 cup plus 2 tablespoons
　margarine, soft　　　　　flour

¾ cup brown sugar　　　½ teaspoon soda

½ teaspoon salt　　　　1 cup rolled oats

1. Combine filling ingredients in a 1-quart bowl. Micro-wave for 4 to 5 minutes at HIGH (100%) until thick and smooth. Stir three times. Set aside.

2. Combine base ingredients in a bowl until crumbly. But-ter may need to be microwaved for 20 seconds at HIGH (100%) first until soft.

3. Press all but 1 cup of the crumbly mixture into an 8x8-inch microwave pan.

*4. Microwave for 3½ to 4½ minutes at MEDIUM (50%) or until done.

5. Spoon filling over base. Sprinkle with remaining 1 cup crumbly mixture.

*6. Microwave for 5 to 7 minutes at HIGH (100%) until crumbly mixture is cooked. Cool and cut into bars.

Yields: 24 bars.

· ❄ ·

* Rotate dish twice, if necessary, for even cooking.

RICE KRISPIES TREATS

· · · · ·

¼ cup margarine or butter
5 cups miniature or 40
  large marshmallows

4½ to 5 cups Rice Krispies
  or other crisp rice cereal
1 cup butterscotch chips
  (optional)

1. Microwave margarine in a 2-quart microwave bowl for 25 seconds at HIGH (100%) until melted. (Add butterscotch chips, if desired, with the butter.)

2. Stir in the marshmallows. Microwave for 1 minute at MEDIUM HIGH (70%). Stir. Microwave again for 1 to 1½ minutes at MEDIUM HIGH (70%) until marshmallows are soft. Stir until smooth.

3. Add cereal and mix thoroughly.

4. Press into a greased 8x12-inch pan. Cool and cut into squares.

Yields: 24 bars.

· ❄ ·

Compacts: Follow same instructions using HIGH (100%) power.

TIPS
· · · · ·

This old-time favorite can be made in minutes in the microwave oven. The butterscotch chips add the special touch, although chocolate chips or raisins may be substituted for them.

You may use frozen rhu-
barb in this recipe. Keep it
frozen until preparation
time, then simply micro-
wave for 2½ to 3 minutes
at HIGH (100%) before
layering.

See shielding section on
pages 9 and 10 for tips on
shielding.

EASY RHUBARB BARS or DUMP CAKE

· · · · ·

Easiest recipe ever for rhubarb.

5 cups diced rhubarb	18-ounce package cake
1 cup sugar	mix (strawberry, white,
1 package cherry Jello	or yellow), dry
	⅓ cup butter, sliced

1. Layer all ingredients in a 8x12-inch microwave dish in order listed. Distribute each layer evenly.

2. Microwave covered with a paper towel for 10 to 12 minutes at HIGH (100%) with corners shielded with foil for the first 8 minutes.

3. Cool 1 hour before serving; the Jello will help set the rhubarb. Delicious served with whipped topping or ice cream.

Yields: 16 bars.

· ❋ ·

S'MORES

· · · · ·

*Now you can make that favorite campfire treat in seconds
in the microwave.*

8 graham cracker squares   4 large marshmallows
1 chocolate candy bar

1. Place 4 graham crackers on a paper towel. Top each with
¼ chocolate bar, 1 marshmallow, and 1 graham cracker.
2. Microwave for 30 to 40 seconds at HIGH (100%) until
marshmallows puff. (1 S'More takes 15 to 20 seconds at HIGH
(100%). 2 S'Mores take 25 to 30 seconds at HIGH (100%).)
Press on crackers lightly to spread marshmallows. Let stand 30
seconds for chocolate to melt.

Yields: 4 S'Mores.

· ❄ ·

Variation: For peanut butter S'Mores, spread each graham
cracker with peanut butter in step #1. Proceed as directed.

· ·

*In marriage it's not as important to pick the right person as to be the
right person.*

This favorite childhood
campfire treat has moved
indoors. Children of all
ages will still ask for "some
more."

Any crushed cereal flakes
may be substituted for the
cornflakes.

CHOCOLATE–PEANUT BUTTER NO-BAKE COOKIES

· · · · ·

A food the kids like to make.

1 cup chocolate chips
1 cup peanut butter chips
1 tablespoon margarine or
   butter

½ cup raisins
5 cups cornflakes, crushed
   to 2⅓ cups

1. Combine both chips and margarine in a 2-quart bowl. Microwave for 2 to 3 minutes at MEDIUM HIGH (70%) until soft. Stir until melted and smooth.

2. Stir in cornflakes and raisins, and mix thoroughly.

3. Drop by teaspoonfuls onto a waxed paper–covered tray. Refrigerate until firm.

Yields: 3½ dozen cookies.

· ❄ ·

OATMEAL FUDGIES

———— · · · · · ————

Fast cookies that require no individual baking.

2 cups sugar
½ cup margarine
1 teaspoon vanilla
½ cup milk

¼ cup cocoa
½ cup peanut butter
3 cups oatmeal (quick)

1. In a 2-quart bowl, combine sugar, margarine, vanilla, milk, and cocoa.

2. Microwave for 3 to 4 minutes at HIGH (100%) until mixture comes to a boil and boils for 1 minute.

3. Stir in peanut butter until smooth. Stir in oatmeal.

4. Drop by teaspoonfuls onto waxed paper.

Yields: 3 dozen cookies.

———— · ❄ · ————

· ·

Some hearts, like primroses, open more beautifully in the shadows of life.

Allow about an hour for the Oatmeal Fudgies to set up.

MADELINE'S PEANUT BUTTER FUDGIES

· · · · ·

14-ounce can sweetened
  condensed milk
¼ cup margarine
2 cups (12 ounces) peanut
  butter chips

½ cup chopped peanuts
1 cup (6 ounces) semi-
  sweet chocolate chips

1. Microwave 1 cup sweetened condensed milk and 2 tablespoons margarine for 3 to 4 minutes at MEDIUM HIGH (70%) until almost boiling. Stir in peanut butter chips until they are melted. Stir in peanuts. Spread into a greased 8- or 9-inch square pan.

2. Microwave remaining sweetened condensed milk and margarine for 2 to 3 minutes at MEDIUM HIGH (70%) until almost boiling. Stir in chocolate chips until melted. Spread chocolate mixture on top of peanut mixture. Cool until firm. Cut into squares.

Yields: 2 dozen squares or 2 pounds.

· ❄ ·

SUGAR COOKIES

———— · · · · · ————

1 cup margarine or butter	¼ teaspoon salt
1½ cups powdered sugar	1 teaspoon vanilla
2 eggs	candied sprinkles,
3 cups flour	frosting, or powdered
1 teaspoon cream of tartar	sugar (optional)
¾ teaspoon baking soda	

1. Using a mixer or food processor, cream butter and powdered sugar until fluffy. Beat in eggs until well blended. Stir in remaining ingredients. Chill at least ½ hour or freeze and use as needed.

2. Shape dough into 1-inch balls and place on waxed paper covering a microwave tray or a piece of cardboard cut to fit the microwave.

3. Flatten balls with a glass dipped in water, then sugar. Cookies should be spaced 1 inch apart.

4. Microwave 9 cookies for 4 to 5 minutes at MEDIUM (50%). Four cookies take only 2 to 3 minutes at MEDIUM (50%).

Yields: 3 dozen.

———— · ❄ · ————

Variation: For slice-and-bake cookies, in step #2 roll dough into 2 rolls, 2 inches in diameter, and freeze. Slice ¼ inch thick, as needed, and microwave as directed.

· ·

Just think how happy you would be if you lost everything you have right now—and then found it again.

Like most sugar cookies, these cookies taste best when frosted with Buttercream Frosting and sprinkled with candied sprinkles. Frost after the cookies are cooled.

— · · · · · —

½ cup margarine	¼ teaspoon salt
1 egg	½ cup chopped nuts
1 teaspoon vanilla	1 package chocolate
⅓ cup powdered sugar	kisses (24)
1¼ cups flour	powdered sugar for
	garnish

1. Microwave margarine in a 2-quart microwave bowl for 25 to 30 seconds at HIGH (100%) until melted.

2. Beat in egg, vanilla, and sugar. Blend in flour, salt, and nuts.

3. Shape dough, the size of a walnut, around each un-wrapped kiss—maintaining the shape of the kiss.

*4. Place 12 at a time on a piece of cardboard or paper plate covered with waxed paper or a paper towel. Microwave for 2 to 2½ minutes at HIGH (100%).

5. Sprinkle with powdered sugar.

Yields: 24 kisses.

— · ❄ · —

. . . .
*Rotate cardboard, if necessary, for even cooking.

FROSTINGS

· ❄ ·

TIPS
· · · ·

Use this frosting any time you need a delicious chocolate frosting. It works well drizzled on bundt cakes, too.

CHOCOLATE CHIPPER FROSTING

· · · · ·

Easy and tasty frosting for brownies or cake.

· FOR 9-INCH X 13-INCH CAKE OR BARS ·

1½ cups sugar   ⅓ cup milk
⅓ cup butter or margarine   1 cup chocolate chips

· FOR 8-INCH X 8-INCH CAKE OR BARS ·

¾ cup sugar   2½ tablespoons milk
2½ tablespoons butter or   ½ cup chocolate chips
   margarine

1. In a 1-quart microwave bowl, combine sugar, butter, and milk. Microwave for 2 to 3 minutes at HIGH (100%) until mixture boils.

2. Stir in chocolate chips until smooth. Frost cake or brownies immediately.

Yields: frosting for 8x8- or 9x13-inch cake.

· ❄ ·

Trouble seems to be one commodity in which the supply exceeds the demand.

BASIC BUTTERCREAM FROSTING
(WITH SEVEN VARIATIONS)

———— · · · · · ————

T I P S
· · · · ·

2 tablespoons butter
2 tablespoons cream or
   milk

dash of salt
2 cups powdered sugar
½ teaspoon vanilla

One tablespoon of milk may be added to any of these frosting variations to make a quick glaze for drizzling on your favorite bundt cake or bread.

1. In a 2-quart microwave bowl, combine butter, cream, and salt. Microwave for 1 minute at HIGH (100%) or until bubbly.

2. Beat in powdered sugar and vanilla.

Yields: frosting for 8x12-inch cake (top only); or 1 layer cake; or 24 cupcakes; or glaze for 1 bundt cake.

———— · ❄ · ————

VARIATIONS

Lemon Frosting: Add 1 teaspoon grated lemon peel and substitute 1 tablespoon lemon juice for 1 tablespoon of the milk before microwaving.

Chocolate Frosting: Add 3 tablespoons cocoa, 2 tablespoons butter, and 1 tablespoon more cream to the basic recipe before microwaving.

Vanilla Frosting: Add ½ teaspoon more vanilla to the basic recipe.

Butterscotch Frosting: Add ¼ cup brown sugar plus 1 tablespoon butter to the basic recipe before microwaving in step #1.

Butter Pecan Frosting: Microwave ¼ cup chopped pecans with 3 tablespoons butter for 3 minutes at HIGH (100%) or until pecans are browned. Continue with basic recipe in step #1, adding cream and salt and substituting browned butter and pecans for the 2 tablespoons butter.

Peanut Butter Frosting: Substitute peanut butter for butter in the basic recipe.

Cherry Nut Frosting: Substitute 1 tablespoon cherry juice for 1 tablespoon of the milk before microwaving. Add 3 tablespoons chopped maraschino cherries and 2 tablespoons chopped nuts before spreading on the cake.

CREAM CHEESE FROSTING

3-ounce package cream cheese	2 cups powdered sugar
¼ cup margarine	1½ teaspoons vanilla

1. Microwave cream cheese and margarine in a microwave bowl for 45 to 60 seconds at MEDIUM HIGH (70%) until softened but not melted.
2. Add remaining ingredients and beat until fluffy.

Yields: frosting for 1 layer cake or 8x12-inch pan bar.

PIES AND DESSERTS

- Microwave cookie-crumb crusts on MEDIUM HIGH (70%) to set them quickly.

- Use commercially frozen pie crusts by transferring them, while frozen, from foil pans to glass or microwave-safe pie pans.

- **Microwave the pie crust before adding the filling for one-crust pies.**

- **Microwave pie shells for 5 to 7 minutes at MEDIUM HIGH** (70%) until brown spots begin to appear on crusts. Stop microwave immediately when these spots appear so crust will not be overcooked.

- Brush pricked pie crusts with egg yolk to seal prick holes (the last minute of microwaving time) if the pie crust will be filled with a custard-type filling.

- Microwave pumpkin, pecan, and custard pies (because of their "sensitive ingredients") at MEDIUM (50%).

- To prepare one-crust fruit pies, microwave prepared fruit filling, crust, and topping separately at HIGH (100%). Then fill crust and top.

- For the BEST two-crust fruit pie (using un-cooked pie crust) use the combination method: Microwave for 9 to 10 minutes at HIGH (100%). Transfer to your regular preheated oven and bake for 8 to 10 minutes at 425°F. Shield crust during oven baking if edges start to overcook.

- Pudding mixes may be cooked on HIGH (100%) because stabilizers prevent curdling.

- Custard-type desserts with eggs do curdle easily, so they should be cooked on MEDIUM (50%) or MEDIUM HIGH (70%).

- Reheat single servings of pie or desserts by microwaving for 30 to 40 seconds at MEDIUM HIGH (70%) per slice or serving.

GRAHAM CRACKER CRUST OR CHOCOLATE COOKIE CRUST OR VANILLA WAFER CRUST

———— · · · · · ————

⅓ cup margarine or butter (soft)

¼ cup sugar

1⅓ cups crushed graham crackers* (or variations, see below)

1. To soften butter: Microwave for 15 to 20 seconds at HIGH (100%). Mix all ingredients together.

2. Press into a 9-inch microwave pie plate. Microwave for 1 to 1½ minutes at MEDIUM HIGH (70%) to set.

Yields: one 9-inch pie crust.

———— · ❄ · ————

VARIATIONS

Chocolate Cookie Crust: Substitute 1⅓ cups crushed Oreo cookies or chocolate wafers for graham crackers. Omit step #2. Refrigerate 1 hour before filling.

Vanilla Water Crust: Substitute 1⅓ cups crushed vanilla wafers or gingersnaps for graham crackers. Omit step #2. Refrigerate 1 hour before filling.

· ·
*One package of 10 graham crackers will make 1⅓ cups crushed graham crackers.

EASY MICROWAVE PIE CRUSTS

---- · · · · · ----

· BASIC PIE CRUST ·

2 cups flour
⅔ cup shortening (butter-
   flavored tastes great)

1 teaspoon sugar
   (optional)
¼ teaspoon salt
⅓ cup iced water or tea

· FRENCH PASTRY ·

2 cups flour
⅔ cup butter
⅓ cup shortening
dash of sugar

1 teaspoon salt
⅓ cup iced water
1 small egg, beaten and
   mixed with water

1. Blend flour, (butter for pastry), shortening, sugar, and salt together until mixture is very crumbly. Use a food processor to save time.

2. Add iced water or tea (plus egg for pastry). Mix until dough forms a ball.

3. Divide in half and refrigerate at least 15 minutes.

4. Roll out pie crust to fit a 9-inch microwave pie plate. Flute edges and prick bottom and sides to prevent bubbling when cooking. Place on an inverted saucer in the microwave.

5. Microwave for 6 to 8 minutes at **MEDIUM HIGH (70%)** or just until brown spots appear, rotating pie plate twice.

Yields: two 9-inch crusts.

---- · ❄ · ----

Compacts: Microwave for 5 to 7 minutes at **HIGH (100%)** in step #5.

Two to three drops of yellow food coloring (for either recipe) enhances the color of the crust.

A mild iced tea may be used instead of water to enhance the color of the crust.

If pie crust will be filled with a liquid/custard-type filling, brush crust with beaten egg yolk to seal prick holes the last minute of microwave cooking time.

Placing the pie plate on an inverted saucer in the microwave oven will help the bottom of the crust cook evenly.

For a perfectly fluted edge, reshape the edge every 2 minutes of microwaving time (because the crust puffs more in a microwave oven than in a conventional oven).

Watch your timing on this peanut butter lover's dessert. Microwave only until the filling starts to boil. The filling will set up as the pie cools.

MOM'S PEANUT BUTTER PIE

——— · · · · · ———

Takes only 5 minutes in the microwave!

· PIE ·

9-inch Basic Pie Crust or Graham Cracker Crust (see pages 109 and 110)
¾ cup sugar
2½ tablespoons cornstarch

2 eggs, well beaten
2 cups milk
⅔ cup peanut butter
1 teaspoon vanilla

· GARNISH ·

½ cup chopped salted peanuts

whipped topping

1. Prepare pie crust.
2. Mix sugar, cornstarch, eggs, and milk in a 2-quart bowl. Microwave for 4 minutes at HIGH (100%). Stir. Microwave again for 1 to 2 minutes at MEDIUM HIGH (70%) or until boiling.
3. Stir in peanut butter and vanilla. Let stand 5 minutes. Pour into a cooled pie crust. Refrigerate. Top with dollops of whipped topping and sprinkle with peanuts before serving.

Yields: one 9-inch pie.

——— · ❄ · ———

Compacts: Microwave for 3 to 4 minutes at HIGH (100%) during second microwave time in step #1.

PECAN PIE

————— ····· —————

9-inch Basic Pie Crust,   ⅓ cup brown sugar
   baked (see page 110)   2 tablespoons flour
¼ cup margarine or butter   1 teaspoon vanilla
3 eggs   1½ cups pecan halves
1 cup dark corn syrup

1. Prepare pie crust.

2. Melt margarine in a 2-quart microwave bowl for 30 to 40 seconds at HIGH (100%). Add eggs. Beat well with a fork or whisk. Stir in syrup, sugar, flour, and vanilla. Microwave for 4 minutes at HIGH (100%).

3. Add pecans. Pour into crust. Microwave for 8 to 12 minutes at MEDIUM (50%) or until top is dry and puffed. Cool.

Yields: one 9-inch pie.

————— · ❄ · —————

TIPS

·····

Be sure to use the ME-DIUM (50%) power setting to allow this pie time to set without overcooking.

LARRY'S FAVORITE
CHOCOLATE CREAM PIE

————— ····· —————

It's rich but delicious!

9-inch Graham Cracker   3½-ounce package instant
   Crust (see page 109)   chocolate pudding
1 package (1 tablespoon)   1½ cups cool whipped
   unflavored gelatin   topping
1½ cups milk   1½ cups vanilla ice cream
½ cup chocolate chips

1. Prepare pie crust. Chocolate chips or chocolate curls for garnish (optional).

2. Sprinkle gelatin on ½ cup milk in a small dish. Stir. Microwave for 1½ to 2 minutes at HIGH (100%). Add choco-

This is my husband's favorite pie, but it is also very rich. Omitting the ice cream and using 3 cups of cool whipped topping makes it a bit lighter.

late chips and stir until melted. (Microwave 1 minute longer if necessary to melt chips.)

3. Prepare pudding with 1 cup milk. Gradually blend in the chocolate mixture, beating until smooth.

4. Fold in whipped topping and ice cream (or 3 cups of either one of them).

5. Spoon into pie crust and refrigerate. Serve topped with whipped topping and garnished with chocolate chips or chocolate curls, if desired.

Yields: one 9-inch pie.

———— · ❄ · ————

T I P S
· · · ·

Try garnishing each slice with a dollop of cool whipped topping, a chocolate curl (shaved from a chocolate bar), and a broken piece of peppermint candy cane for holiday entertaining.

One cup whipping cream, whipped, may be substituted for the 1½ cups cool whipped topping.

GRASSHOPPER PIE

———— · · · · · ————

A jiffy but elegant after-dinner dessert.

9-inch Chocolate Cookie Crust (see page 109)
32 large marshmallows
½ cup cream or milk
2 tablespoons green creme de menthe

2 tablespoons creme de cacao
5 drops green food coloring (optional)
1½ cups cool whipped topping

1. Prepare pie crust.

2. In a 2-quart microwave bowl, combine marshmallows and milk. Microwave for 2 to 3 minutes at HIGH (100%). Marshmallows will look puffy. Stir until mixture is smooth.

3. Stir in liqueurs and food coloring. Chill 10 minutes or until mixture resembles egg whites in consistency.

4. Fold whipped topping into marshmallow mixture.

5. Pour into crust.

6. Freeze 3 to 4 hours. Transfer to refrigerator ½ hour before serving.

Yields: one 9-inch pie.

———— · ❄ · ————

EASY FRESH STRAWBERRY PIE (GLACÉ)

9-inch Basic Pie Crust (see
  page 110)
1 quart strawberries
1 cup sugar
½ cup water

3 tablespoons cornstarch
2 teaspoons lemon juice
1 cup whipped topping
  for garnish

1. Prepare pie crust.
2. Mash 1 cup of berries in a 2-quart microwave-safe bowl and refrigerate remainder.
3. Add sugar and ¼ cup water to the mashed berries. Microwave at HIGH (100%) for 3 to 4 minutes until boiling.
4. Combine cornstarch and ¼ cup water in a separate dish. Add to boiling mixture. Microwave at HIGH (100%) for 2 to 3 minutes until thick. Refrigerate.
5. Before serving, fold in lemon juice and remaining berries.
6. Pour into pie crust. Top with whipped topping.

Yields: one 9-inch pie.

TIPS

Try serving each slice topped with whipped topping and a chocolate-tipped strawberry. To tip the strawberry: Microwave ½ cup chocolate chips and 1 teaspoon vegetable oil for 1 minute at MEDIUM HIGH (70%). Stir until smooth. Dip each strawberry (with stem attached) into the melted chocolate until partially coated. Chill on a waxed paper—lined tray until ready to serve.

TIPS
· · · ·

For 2 teaspoons pumpkin pie spice you may substitute: 1 teaspoon cinnamon, ½ teaspoon nutmeg, ¼ teaspoon ginger, and ⅛ teaspoon allspice.

The baked pie crust should be brushed with beaten egg yolk to seal prick holes.

If you have a convection microwave oven, use the convection microwave variation. Three settings are suggested. Choose the one that corresponds to the power setting on your convection microwave.

PUMPKIN PIE
· · · · ·

The old-fashioned recipe cooked the new-fashioned way.

9-inch Basic Pie Crust or Vanilla Wafer Crust (see pages 109 and 110)
2 large eggs
1 cup brown sugar
2 tablespoons flour

2 teaspoons pumpkin pie spice
1 cup evaporated milk
16-ounce can or 2 cups mashed, cooked pumpkin

1. Prepare pie crust.
2. Combine all ingredients, except crust, in a microwave-safe bowl. Beat until smooth. Microwave for 8 minutes at MEDIUM (50%), stirring often.
3. Pour into pie crust. Microwave for 25 to 32 minutes at MEDIUM (50%) or until center is set but looks slightly moist. Let stand 10 minutes.

Yields: one 9-inch pie.

─── · ❄ · ───

Variations for a brown crust: In step #2, microwave for 8 minutes at HIGH (100%) and bake in your preheated oven at 450°F. for 20 minutes. (You may use an unbaked pie shell.)
Convection Microwave: Convection Microwave Low-Mix Bake at 350°F. OR Combination #2 OR Code #2 for 25 to 30 minutes. (You may use an unbaked pie shell.)

Some women like to travel, while others like a book; but the woman who will get her man, is the one who likes to cook.

KATIE SCANLIN'S ICE CREAM FUDGE PIE

———— · · · · · ————

It's rich and delicious so one pie will serve many.

9-inch Chocolate Cookie
  Crust (see page 109)
1 cup evaporated milk
1 cup chocolate chips

1 cup miniature marsh-
  mallows
¼ teaspoon salt
1 quart vanilla ice cream
½ cup pecan halves

To prevent overcooking the chips and marshmallows: Stir well after 3 minutes of microwaving; add microwaving time in 1-minute increments, as needed.

1. Prepare pie crust.

2. Combine milk, chocolate chips, marshmallows, and salt in a 2-quart microwave bowl.

3. Microwave for 3 to 5 minutes at HIGH (100%), stirring occasionally until chips and marshmallows melt and mixture begins to thicken. Cool to room temperature.

4. Spoon 2 cups ice cream into chocolate crust.

5. Cover with half of the chocolate mixture.

6. Repeat with remaining ice cream and chocolate.

7. Decorate with pecan halves and freeze until firm.

Yields: 8 to 10 servings.

———— · ❄ · ————

When work seems rather dull to me and life is not so sweet, one thing at least can bring me joy, I simply love to eat.

APPLE CRISP WITH VARIATIONS

——— · · · · · ———

Delicious with ice cream or whipped cream!

6 cups peeled, cored, and sliced apples
1 tablespoon lemon juice
⅓ cup white sugar
⅔ cup rolled oats
¼ cup flour

⅔ cup brown sugar
1 teaspoon cinnamon
¼ cup butter or margarine, soft
dash of nutmeg

1. Combine apples, lemon juice, and white sugar in an 8x8-inch baking dish. Microwave for 2 minutes at HIGH (100%).

2. Combine remaining ingredients until crumbly. Sprinkle evenly over hot apples. Shield the corners with foil.

3. Microwave again for 9 to 12 minutes at HIGH (100%) until apples are tender. Remove foil shielding last 5 minutes. Cool.

Yields: 12 servings.

——— · ❄ · ———

VARIATIONS

Substitute 1 can cherry or peach pie filling or 5 cups peaches for the apples for a fruit crisp of your choice. Follow the directions listed above. (Omit white sugar if using the pie filling.)

MOM'S STRAWBERRY PRETZEL DESSERT

· · · · ·

· CRUST ·

1 stick margarine (½ cup)   3 tablespoons sugar
1⅔ cups crushed pretzels

· FILLING ·

8-ounce package cream   9-ounce package cool
  cheese   whipped topping
1 cup sugar or 1⅓ cups
  powdered sugar

· GELATIN ·

2 cups hot water   20-ounce frozen or 1 pint
6-ounce package (or two   fresh strawberries (with
  3-ounce packages)   or without sugar syrup)
  strawberry gelatin

1. **For crust:** Microwave margarine in an 8x12-inch microwave pan or dish for 30 to 40 seconds at HIGH (100%) until melted. Stir in pretzels and sugar. Reserve ¼ cup pretzel mixture for garnish. Press remainder into the dish. Microwave for 3 to 3½ minutes at HIGH (100%) or until center bubbles. Cool.

2. **For filling:** Microwave cheese in a 1-quart bowl for 40 seconds at MEDIUM HIGH (70%) until soft. Stir in sugar. Stir in whipped topping. Spread over crust.

3. Microwave water in the 1-quart bowl for 2 minutes at HIGH (100%) or until boiling. Stir in gelatin. Stir in frozen strawberries. (If using fresh strawberries, allow mixture to partially set before stirring in strawberries.) Allow mixture to partially set and then spread over cheese filling and refrigerate. Garnish with remaining pretzel mixture and cut into squares.

Yields: 12 to 16 servings.

——— · ❄ · ———

TIPS
· · · · ·

Presweetened frozen strawberries make this dessert sweeter, but fresh strawberries work well, too. If using fresh whole strawberries, rinse, detach stems, and slice before adding to the partially set gelatin.

You may substitute any flavor pudding mix for the vanilla pudding, but it must be the kind that requires cooking. You do not need to cover the pudding while microwaving.

EASY RICE PUDDING

———— · · · · · ————

2 cups milk
½ cup Minute Rice
½ cup raisins

3¾-ounce package vanilla
   pudding (not instant)

1. Combine all ingredients in a 1-quart casserole. Microwave for 5 to 6 minutes at HIGH (100%). Stir twice while cooking.

2. Pour into serving dishes. Chill.

Yields: 3 to 4 servings.

———— · ❄ · ————

Do not double the recipe in one mug as it may boil over while microwaving. If you double the recipe, use two mugs.

Top pudding with a sliced banana for a special treat.

CHOCOLATE PUDDING FOR ONE OR TWO
(IN A MUG OR LARGE CUSTARD CUP)

———— · · · · · ————

1 tablespoon sugar
1 tablespoon cornstarch
¾ cup milk

3 tablespoons chocolate
   chips
½ teaspoon vanilla

1. Mix sugar and cornstarch in a mug that is microwave safe. Stir in milk, mixing until smooth.

2. Microwave for 2 to 3 minutes at HIGH (100%) until boiling.

3. Stir in chocolate chips and vanilla until smooth.

Yields: 1 serving.

———— · ❄ · ————

For two mugs: Microwave for 4 to 5 minutes at HIGH (100%).

SIMPLY EASY CHEESECAKE

— · · · · · —

T I P S
· · · · ·

The Simply Easy Cheese-
cake will not look firm in
the center after microwaving. It will set up when
cooled.

9-inch Graham Cracker
   Crust (see page 109)
8 ounces cream cheese
½ cup sugar

1 egg
1 teaspoon vanilla
1 can cherry pie filling

1. Soften cream cheese by microwaving for 40 to 50 seconds
at MEDIUM HIGH (70%).

2. Beat cream cheese, sugar, egg, and vanilla until well
blended. Pour into crust (in a microwave-safe pan).

3. Microwave for 4 to 6 minutes at MEDIUM HIGH
(70%).

4. Cool and spread with cherry pie filling before serving.

Yields: 6 to 8 servings.

——— · ❄ · ———

Variation: For chocolate swirl cheesecake, reserve ⅓ of the
cream cheese mixture before pouring into the crust. Beat 1
tablespoon cocoa into the reserved mixture and drizzle onto
filling and swirl with a knife. Continue with step #3.

Refrigerated cream cheese may be softened by removing foil wrapping, and microwaving in a glass bowl for 40 to 60 seconds at MEDIUM HIGH (70%).

The cheesecake will look firm around the edges but soft in the center after microwaving. It will set up in the center during the standing time. If it is overcooked, it will taste tough, not creamy.

FAMOUS CHEESECAKE

· · · · ·

· FILLING ·

3 medium eggs | 1 teaspoon vanilla
12 ounces cream cheese, soft | ½ cup sugar

· CRUST ·

9-inch Graham Cracker Crust* (see page 109) in a microwave pan or pie plate

· TOPPING ·

1½ cups sour cream | 1 teaspoon vanilla
2 tablespoons sugar

1. Using a blender, food processor, or mixer, combine the filling ingredients until smooth.

2. Pour into crust. Microwave at MEDIUM (50%) for 10 to 12 minutes or until center is almost set. Cool 30 minutes.

3. Combine topping ingredients as in #1. Carefully spread on top of cake.

4. Microwave again at MEDIUM (50%) for 3 to 4 minutes. Let stand 5 to 10 minutes. Refrigerate. Garnish with crumbs from the Graham Cracker Crust.

Yields: 8 to 10 servings.

——— · ❊ · ———

* Save a few crumbs for garnishing.

BAKED CUSTARD FOR ONE OR TWO

— — · · · · · — —

A quick and easy treat.

1 cup milk	½ teaspoon vanilla
3 tablespoons sugar	dash cinnamon or nutmeg
2 eggs	

1. Microwave milk in a 1-cup measure for 1½ to 2 minutes at HIGH (100%) until bubbly.

2. Mix sugar, eggs, and vanilla in a small bowl. Stir in milk.

3. Divide into two 6-ounce custard cups or mugs. Sprinkle with spice.

*4. Microwave for 3 to 4½ minutes at MEDIUM HIGH (70%) until custard is soft set like gelatin. Cool—center will become firm.

Yields: 2 servings.

— — · ❄ · — —

For 4 servings: Double the recipe. Microwave for 4 to 7½ minutes at MEDIUM HIGH (70%).

· ·

*Rotate dishes, if necessary, for even cooking.

T I P S
· · · ·

If red baking cups are not available, use pink ones and turn the edges back after filling to create a ruffled effect.

CHEESECAKE CUPS

—— · · · · · ——

Great for holiday entertaining—serve in red baking cups.

· CUPS ·

6 vanilla wafers

12 baking cups

8-ounce package cream cheese

⅓ cup brown sugar

1 egg

1 teaspoon vanilla

· TOPPING ·

½ can cherry pie filling or
  ¼ cup sour cream and 6
  large strawberries

1. Place 2 medium-size paper baking cups in each cup of a microwave muffin pan or in 6 custard cups. Place a vanilla wafer in each cup. Set aside.

2. Microwave cream cheese in a 2-quart microwave bowl for 1 to 2 minutes at DEFROST (30%) until soft. Stir in brown sugar, egg, and vanilla and beat until smooth.

3. Pour into baking cups. Microwave 6 cups for 7 to 8 minutes at DEFROST (30%).

4. Remove paper baking cups from dish(es). Cool at least 1 hour. Garnish with cherry pie filling and/or sour cream and sugar-sprinkled strawberries before serving. Keep refrigerated.

Yields: 6 servings.

—— · · ——

PUDDING FROM A MIX

— · · · · · —

3½-ounce package pudding mix (not instant)

2 cups milk or as package directs

1. Prepare mix according to package directions in a 2-quart microwave-safe bowl or casserole.
2. Microwave for 3 minutes at HIGH (100%). Stir. Microwave again for 2 to 4 minutes at MEDIUM HIGH (70%) until mixture boils.
3. Chill. Mixture thickens when cooled.

Yields: 4 servings.

——— · ❋ · ———

Compacts: Microwave for 3 to 4 minutes at HIGH (100%) during second microwave time in step #2.

EGGS AND BREAKFAST FOODS

· · · · ·

- **Do not microwave eggs in the shell**—they will EXPLODE (the yolk cooks quickly and causes pressure against the shell).

- Always cover whole eggs to seal in the moisture and keep the yolk from becoming tough.

- **For hard-cooked eggs for potato salads, etc.:** Microwave eggs in buttered individual custard cups. Prick yolk and white with a fork twice and cover with a small piece of waxed paper. Microwave for 1½ to 2 minutes at MEDIUM (50%) or until white is set. Let stand 1 minute. For 2 eggs: microwave for 2½ to 3 minutes at MEDIUM (50%).

- **For easy "No-Cleanup" scrambled eggs:** Microwave 1 egg in a Styrofoam cup for 35 to 50 seconds at HIGH (100%). (See recipe on page 128.)

- **For poached eggs:** Microwave 2 tablespoons water and ¼ teaspoon vinegar in a custard cup until boiling. Add 1 egg and microwave for 30 to 45 seconds at MEDIUM HIGH (70%). Let stand 1 minute and remove. (See recipe on page 131.)

- **For quiches:** Microwave the pastry shell first (unless a baking mix recipe that requires no shell is used) and then pour in the egg mixture. Quiches are microwaved for about 30 minutes at MEDIUM (50%).

- **For oatmeal or cream of wheat:** No need to use instant cereal or even heat the water first. Simply mix 1 cup water for every ½ cup cereal in a 2-quart bowl. Microwave for 3 to 4 minutes at HIGH (100%). (See recipe on page 127.)

- **For homemade granola:** Use your favorite recipe and microwave 5 cups of ingredients for 7 to 8 minutes at HIGH (100%), stirring often. (See recipe on page 127.)

Responsible children (eight years old or older) can learn to make cream of wheat or oatmeal for themselves.

Be sure to use a large bowl as the cereal boils up while cooking.

If stored in the refrigerator, this granola will keep for over a month.

OATMEAL OR CREAM OF WHEAT
(REGULAR AND QUICK)*

———— . . . . . ————

oatmeal or cream of wheat (⅓ cup per serving)

water (2 times the quantity of cereal, ⅔ cup per serving)

1. Place oatmeal and water in a 2-quart bowl. (It boils up so use a tall bowl.) Cook up to 3 to 4 servings at once.

2. Microwave for 3 to 4 minutes at HIGH (100%) for 1 to 3 servings. (Microwave for 4 to 5 minutes at HIGH (100%) for 4 or more servings.) Let stand 2 minutes. Serve with raisins, brown sugar, and milk. Enjoy!

. . . .

*You may use either regular or quick-cooking cereal. Do not use instant. For quick cereals, reduce time by 1 minute.

GRANOLA

———— . . . . . ————

¼ cup margarine or salad oil

¼ cup honey

¼ cup brown sugar

2½ cups oatmeal (dry)

½ cup chopped nuts or seeds or almonds

3 tablespoons bran or wheat germ

2 teaspoons vanilla

½ cup raisins

1. In a 2-quart (flat) casserole combine margarine, honey, and brown sugar. Microwave for 1 to 1½ minutes at HIGH (100%) until everything is melted. Stir well. Mix in oatmeal, nuts, and bran.

2. Microwave for 7 to 8 minutes at HIGH (100%), stirring every 2 to 3 minutes to prevent burning.

3. Stir in vanilla and raisins. Cool, cover, and store.

Yields: 4 cups.

———— · ❄ · ————

SCRAMBLED EGGS OR EGG OMELET
IN A STYROFOAM CUP

———— · · · · · ————

Easy "no-cleanup" breakfast.

8- to 10-ounce Styrofoam   salt and pepper to taste
  cup   1 tablespoon water or
1–2 large eggs   milk

1. Break egg(s) into the cup. Add seasonings and water or milk.
2. Whip with a fork.
3. Microwave 1 egg for 25 seconds at HIGH (100%). Stir. Microwave again for 15 to 20 seconds at HIGH (100%). Let stand 1 minute to firm (while you make the toast). For two eggs: Microwave 30 seconds, stir. Microwave again for 25 to 35 seconds at HIGH (100%).
4. Eat, enjoy, and throw away the cup for easy cleanup.

Yields: 1 serving.

———— · ❄ · ————

Variation: For a low-calorie cheesy omelet, stir in 1 tablespoon cottage cheese per egg and microwave 10 seconds longer after stirring. Top with 1 slice low-fat processed cheese during standing time.

T I P S
· · · · ·

Dieters may find the low-calorie cheesy omelet variation quite appealing and filling.

· ·
Think a minute—do you really want your children to be just like you?

BROCCOLI SOUFFLÉ

───── · · · · · ─────

A great light lunch idea.

16-ounce package frozen chopped broccoli	2 cups grated brick cheese
3 eggs, beaten	1½ cups cottage cheese
3 tablespoons flour	dash salt and pepper (optional)

1. Microwave broccoli in the bag for 9 minutes at HIGH (100%). (Pierce bag first and place on a paper towel.) Drain well.

2. Combine beaten eggs and flour in a 2-quart casserole. Mix until smooth. Stir in all ingredients including broccoli.

3. Microwave for 20 to 25 minutes at MEDIUM (50%) until almost set in center (200°F.). Let stand 5 minutes.

Yields: 4 servings.

───── · ❉ · ─────

Variation: Substitute spinach for broccoli.

. . . .

Middle age is that period in life when our broad mind and narrow waist begin to exchange places.

CHICKEN BROCCOLI QUICHE

—— · · · · · ——

Serve with a salad for an easy luncheon.

10-ounce package frozen
   chopped broccoli
1 cup cubed cooked
   chicken
2 tablespoons chopped
   onion (optional)

1½ cups shredded
   cheddar cheese
3 eggs
1 cup milk
½ cup baking mix (like
   Bisquick)
½ teaspoon seasoned salt

· TOPPING ·

⅓ cup baking mix
¼ cup chopped nuts
2 tablespoons margarine

¼ cup grated Parmesan
   cheese
½ teaspoon paprika

1. Cook broccoli in the box for 5 minutes at HIGH (100%). Let stand 2 minutes. Drain.

2. Layer chicken, onion, broccoli, and cheese in a 9-inch microwave pie plate.

3. Mix eggs, milk, baking mix, and seasoned salt using a mixer, blender, or food processor.

4. Pour over top of chicken, broccoli, and cheese.

5. Mix topping ingredients and crumble on top of quiche.

*6. Microwave for 6 minutes at HIGH (100%). Microwave again for 4 to 6 minutes at MEDIUM (50%) until almost set.

7. Let stand 5 minutes. Cut into wedges. Serve topped with a slice of tomato for a garnish, if desired.

Yields: 6 servings.

—— · ❈ · ——

Compacts: Microwave for 13 to 15 minutes at HIGH (100%) in step #6.

· ·
* Rotate twice if necessary for even cooking.

For the cubed chicken, you may use two 6½-ounce cans of cooked chicken or see the recipe for Poaching Chicken, page 187.

Quiches cook best when started at HIGH (100%) and finished at MEDIUM (50%). If cooked at HIGH (100%) throughout the microwaving time, the edges will become tough before the center gets done.

The center of the quiche will finish cooking during the standing time.

You will NOT taste the vinegar. The vinegar helps the whites coagulate or set.

Use a Styrofoam or custard cup for easy cleanup.

2 tablespoons water per egg
1–4 eggs

¼ teaspoon vinegar per egg

1. Place water and vinegar in a Styrofoam, custard, or muffin cup for each egg. Microwave for ½ to 1½ minutes at HIGH (100%) until boiling.

2. Break 1 egg into each cup. Prick yolk with a fork. Cover with waxed paper. **For 1 egg:** Microwave for 30 to 45 seconds at MEDIUM HIGH (70%). **For 2 eggs:** Microwave for 45 to 60 seconds at MEDIUM HIGH (70%). **For 3 eggs:** Microwave for 1 to 1½ minutes at MEDIUM HIGH (70%). **For 4 eggs:** Microwave for 1½ to 2½ minutes at MEDIUM HIGH (70%). Let stand 1 minute and remove immediately to prevent overcooking. (You may microwave 4 eggs in a 1-quart casserole with 1 cup boiling water and ½ teaspoon vinegar instead of the individual cups. Follow same cooking time as above.)

———— · ❋ · ————

Pray for a good harvest, but continue to hoe.

SAUSAGE BREAKFAST FRITTATA

— · · · · · —

Easy breakfast or brunch idea!

8–12 ounces bulk
  sausage,
  crumbled
1 cup shredded cheddar
  cheese
2 tablespoons finely sliced
  green onion

4 eggs, beaten
1 cup evaporated milk
dash salt
1 tablespoon chopped
  parsley

1. Microwave sausage in a 9-inch microwave pie plate (covered with a paper towel) for 4 to 5 minutes on HIGH (100%) until no longer pink. Drain well.

2. Sprinkle cheese over sausage and add green onion.

3. Beat eggs with milk, salt, and parsley in a medium bowl.

*4. Pour into the pie plate. Cover with plastic wrap. Microwave for 4 minutes at HIGH (100%). Stir. Microwave again for 7 to 8 minutes at MEDIUM (50%) or until center is set but not dry, stirring once during cooking. Let stand 5 minutes.

Yields: 6 servings.

— · ❄ · —

T I P S
· · · · ·

A frittata is a quiche without the crust (and without the calories in the crust).

· ·

* Rotate plate during microwaving for even cooking.

A quick breakfast idea for six! Use your convection microwave or use your range with your microwave. If you do not own a convection microwave, you can get similar results by using your microwave first and then transferring the strata to your conventional oven.

Three convection microwave settings are suggested. Choose the one that corresponds to the power setting on your convection microwave oven.

HAM AND CHEESE SOUFFLÉ OR STRATA

———— · · · · · ————

The perfect brunch main dish—make it the night before.

8 slices bread	2 cups milk
(trim crusts and cube)	½ teaspoon salt
1 cup grated sharp	1 cup crushed cornflakes
cheddar cheese	or other cereal
1 cup grated Swiss cheese	1 tablespoon butter, sliced
¼ pound ham, cubed	paprika
4 eggs	

1. Liberally butter an 8x8-inch or 6x10-inch baking dish. Place half of the bread cubes in the dish. Sprinkle with half of the cheeses and all of the ham. Repeat with remaining bread and cheese.

2. Beat eggs with milk and salt. Pour over cheese. Cover with plastic wrap. Refrigerate overnight.

3. Sprinkle with cereal and butter. **Convection Microwave Low-Mix Bake at 350°F.** (OR Combination #2 OR Code #2) for 20 minutes. Let stand 5 minutes. **OR FOR MICROWAVE AND REGULAR OVEN:** Microwave for 8 to 9 minutes at **HIGH (100%)**; transfer to regular oven (preheated). Bake for 15 minutes at 375°F.

Yields: 6 servings.

———— · ❄ · ————

· ·

We can't take it with us, but perhaps how we got it may determine where we will go.

FOOD PRESERVATION AND JELLIES

· · · · ·

· **Do not try to "can" directly** in a microwave oven. It is not safe for you or the food you will eat. Use conventional preservation methods for sealing jars and freezing foods. However, you may use a specially designed microwave canner, which is available in the accessory department of most department stores. (It will can one pint at a time, every 20 minutes.)

· **Blanching is easy in the microwave oven.** Follow the blanching chart and directions on page 143.

· Jellies and jams made in the microwave taste great and are very time saving. If you have never tried to make homemade jam, please try it! You will be surprised at how easy it is. What a wonderful way to "treat" your family and friends.

· ALWAYS MAKE ONLY THE AMOUNTS OF JELLIES OR JAMS LISTED IN THESE RECIPES. Always use at least a large 2-quart microwave-safe bowl. If you don't—in either case—the jam will boil over onto your microwave oven, which can be very **MESSY!**

- Microwaved jams and jellies will keep up to 4 months in the refrigerator.

- If paraffin is used in sealing jam, **DO NOT MICRO-WAVE THE PARAFFIN.**

- Powdered pectin has always worked best for me in these recipes.

- A 2-quart glass measuring bowl works great for making jellies and for blanching.

- **Lemon juice is an important ingredient in causing your jam to gel.** It helps balance the acid and sugar and the fruit and pectin. Do not eliminate it; it will NOT add a sour flavor.

- **Your microwave oven easily becomes a food dehydrator, too!** Microwave fruit or vegetable slices (¼ inch thick and in a single layer) on a microwave roasting rack for 12 to 15 minutes at MEDIUM (50%) or until limp and moist. Transfer to a wire rack and let stand overnight. (Try apples, bananas, pineapple, apricots, carrots, potatoes, or mushrooms.)

TIPS

· · · ·

A 2-quart measuring bowl with a handle is convenient for cooking jams and jellies. The heated fruit syrup gets very hot while cooking, but the handle stays cool for easy handling.

APPLE JELLY (OR GRAPE, PEAR, PINEAPPLE)

——— · · · · · ———

Pour into a mug or decorative jar for a nice gift.

6-ounce can apple juice concentrate (or grape, pineapple, etc.)

2 cups water
1¾-ounce box powdered pectin
3⅔ cups sugar

1. Combine juice and water in a 2-quart microwave-safe bowl. Stir in pectin until dissolved.
2. Microwave for 10 to 12 minutes at HIGH (100%) or until mixture comes to a boil and boils one minute, stirring every 3 minutes.
3. Stir in sugar.
4. Microwave for 6 to 7 minutes at HIGH (100%) or until mixture returns to a boil and boils for 1 minute (only), stirring twice.
5. Skim off foam. Pour into hot, sterilized jars or mugs. Cover and let stand at room temperature until cool. Refrigerate or freeze.

Yields: 4 cups or 7 to 8 small jars.

——— · ❄ · ———

JAM (FROM FROZEN FRUIT)

2 10-ounce packages
  frozen strawberries
  (raspberries, or
  peaches, etc.)

3 tablespoons plus 2
  teaspoons powdered
  pectin
2⅓ cups sugar
2 teaspoons lemon juice

1. Microwave fruit in a 2- to 3-quart microwave-safe bowl for 2½ minutes at HIGH (100%).

2. Stir in pectin. Microwave for 2 minutes at HIGH (100%) or until bubbly.

3. Stir in sugar and lemon juice.

4. Microwave for 6 minutes at HIGH (100%) or until mixture boils for 1 minute (only). Watch closely.

5. Pour into sterilized jars. Cover and let stand at room temperature until cool. Refrigerate or freeze.

Yields: 3½ cups or 5 to 6 small jars.

APPLE BUTTER
(WITH APRICOT, PEACH, OR PLUM VARIATIONS)

6 cups prepared apples
  (sliced)
½ cup apple cider
1¼ cups sugar
½ teaspoon ground cloves

¼ teaspoon allspice
1 teaspoon cinnamon
2 teaspoons lemon juice
1 teaspoon grated lemon
  rind (optional)

1. Microwave apple slices and cider in a 2-quart covered microwave-safe bowl for 8 to 10 minutes at HIGH (100%) or until boiling.

2. Stir and microwave again for 7 minutes at MEDIUM (50%).

3. Mash apples with a fork and add remaining ingredients.

4. Microwave, uncovered, for 15 to 18 minutes at HIGH (100%). Stir 2 or 3 times. Mixture should be very thick.

5. Pour into sterilized jars. Cover and let stand at room temperature until cool. Refrigerate or freeze.

Yields: 3 cups.

———— · ❄ · ————

Compacts: Microwave in step #4 for 16 to 20 minutes.

Variations: For apricot, peach, or plum butter, use ½ cup water instead of the cider. Use the same amount of sliced fruit.

STRAWBERRY JAM
You may substitute any fresh fruit.

T I P S
· · · ·
Any fruit may be substituted for the strawberries. Use approximately 1 quart whole berries before crushing.

2 cups fresh prepared and crushed strawberries	2 cups white sugar
3 tablespoons powdered pectin	2 teaspoons lemon juice

1. Crush fruit in a 2-quart bowl with a fork. Microwave for 2 minutes at HIGH (100%).

2. Stir in pectin. Microwave for 2 minutes at HIGH (100%) or until bubbly.

3. Stir in sugar and lemon juice.

4. Microwave for 6 minutes (no longer) at HIGH (100%).

5. Pour into sterilized jars. Cover and let stand at room temperature until cool. Refrigerate or freeze.

Yields: 2½ cups or 3 to 4 small jars.

———— · ❄ · ————

Compacts: Microwave in step #4 for 8 minutes.

RHUBARB JAM

———— · · · · · ————

4 cups thinly sliced rhubarb

2¾ cups sugar

3-ounce box strawberry or raspberry Jello

1. Combine rhubarb and sugar in a 2-quart or larger microwave-safe bowl. Let stand at least 2 hours (overnight is best) so that the rhubarb makes its own juice.

2. Microwave rhubarb-sugar mixture for 15 minutes at HIGH (100%) stirring 3 times while cooking.

3. Stir in Jello. Mix well.

4. Pour into sterilized jars. Cover and let stand at room temperature until cool. Refrigerate or freeze.

Yields: 2½ cups or 3 to 4 small jars.

———— · ❄ · ————

SUGARLESS JAM

———— · · · · · ————

Less than 5 calories per teaspoon—made with sugar substitute. Great for dieters and diabetics.

1 cup crushed berries or fruit *

⅓ cup sugar or equivalent substitute

1 cup apple juice

¼ cup (about 1 ounce dry) Slim Set (by MCP Foods, Inc.)

drop food coloring to enhance color (optional)

1. Combine crushed fruit and sugar substitute. Microwave for 2 minutes at HIGH (100%).

· ·

* Start with washed fruit, approximately 1 pound or 2½ cups before crushing.

I've been making this jam every summer for many years. It may be heated later and served as a topping on angel food cake, cheese cake, ice cream, or pancakes.

You may use 7 packets of Sweet 'n Low or Weight Watchers' sugar substitute for the ⅓ cup sugar.

2. Stir in apple juice. Add Slim Set and coloring if desired and mix well.

3. Microwave for 5 to 6 minutes at HIGH (100%) or until boiling. Microwave for 1 minute at HIGH (100%) while boiling.

4. Skim foam. Pour into sterilized jars. Cover and let stand at room temperature until cool. Refrigerate or freeze.

Yields: 2 cups.

———————— · ❄ · ————————

T I P S
· · · · ·

Do not try to can directly in your microwave oven. The lids will NOT seal.

Preserving large amounts of pickles using the microwave oven is NOT practical because there is no time saving. However, the microwave does save time and is helpful for small batches.

DILL PICKLES

———————— · · · · · ————————

3–6 cloves garlic (½–1 per jar)
6 sprigs fresh dill
3 teaspoons pickling spice (½ teaspoon per jar), optional

40 3-inch cucumbers for pickling, washed and prepared

· BRINE ·

¼ teaspoon alum
3 cups water

1½ cups vinegar
⅓ cup pickling salt

1. Fill sterilized jars with garlic, dill, pickling spice, and cucumbers, divided evenly among the jars. Set aside.

2. Combine brine ingredients in a 2-quart microwave-safe bowl. Microwave for 11 to 12 minutes at HIGH (100%) or until boiling (about 200°F.).

· ·

Happiness adds and multiplies as we divide it with others.

3. Pour brine over cucumbers. Seal using the conventional boiling-water–bath method or refrigerate. If refrigerated, pickles are ready in 1 week and can be kept in the refrigerator for 3 months.

Yields: 6 pints.

———— · ❄ · ————

REFRIGERATOR PICKLES

———— · · · · · ————

7 cups thinly sliced cucumbers (not peeled)	2 cups sugar
1 cup sliced onions	1 cup vinegar
1 cup sliced green pepper (optional)	1 tablespoon celery seed
1 tablespoon pickling salt	1 teaspoon mustard seed (optional)

1. Combine the cucumbers, onion, green pepper, and pickling salt. Cover and let stand 1 hour.

2. Combine sugar, vinegar, and seeds in a 1-quart microwave-safe bowl. Microwave for 8 to 10 minutes at HIGH (100%) or until boiling (200°F.). Cool slightly.

3. Drain cucumbers well. Pour slightly cooled vinegar syrup over cucumbers. Refrigerate in a covered container.

4. Pickles will be ready to eat in 3 days. They may be kept for 4 months in the refrigerator.

Yields: 2 quarts.

———— · ❄ · ————

. . . .

Give others a piece of your heart, not a piece of your mind.

Vegetables tend to dry out if microwaved with salt. You may add salt when you place the vegetables in the freezer bags.

The microwave oven is perfect for blanching small batches. (Not only is it quick but much of the vitamin C in vegetables is retained.) However, when blanching large batches, you will save more time by using the conventional stove-top method.

1. Prepare vegetables as for conventional blanching.

2. Use only the amount of vegetable specified in the chart and place in a microwave-safe dish.

3. Add water as indicated. Do not add salt. Cover with a lid or plastic wrap.

4. Cook on HIGH (100%) for the time listed in the chart.

5. Stir halfway through cooking time.

6. Check for doneness. Vegetables should have an evenly bright color throughout.

7. Plunge into ice water at once.

8. Drain well. Pat dry with paper toweling.

9. Package in freezer containers or freezer-weight plastic bags. Seal. Label, date, and freeze quickly.

Variation: Omit steps 7, 8, and 9; transfer the vegetables, using tongs, to a freezer bag; seal the bag and then immerse the bag in ice water.

VEGETABLE	AMOUNT	MICROWAVE DISH	WATER	MINUTES
Asparagus	1 lb., cut into 1-in. pieces	2 qt.	¼ c.	3 to 4
Beans	1 lb.	1½ qt.	½ c	4 to 6
Broccoli	1 bunch (1¼ to 1½ lb.)	2 qt.	½ c.	4 to 5½
Carrots	1 lb., sliced	1½ qt.	¼ c.	4 to 6
Cauliflower	1 head, cut into flowerets	2 qt.	½ c.	4 to 5½
Corn, cut	4 c.	1½ qt.	¼ c.	4 to 5
Corn on cob	6 ears	8x12-inch dish	none	5½
Onions	4 med., quartered	1 qt.	½ c	3 to 4½
Parsnips	1 lb., cubed	1½ qt.	¼ c.	2½ to 4
Peas	2 lb., shelled	1 qt.	¼ c.	3½ to 5
Spinach	1 lb., washed	2 qt.	none	2½ to 4
Squash, yellow	1 lb., sliced or cubed	1½ qt.	¼ c.	3 to 4½
Turnips	1 lb., cubed	1½ qt.	¼ c.	3 to 4½
Zucchini	1 lb., sliced or cubed	1½ qt.	¼ c.	3 to 4½

FISH

·····

- **A microwave steams, poaches, and bakes fish perfectly** in 75% less time than a conventional oven.

- Use your favorite recipe, but use ¼ less liquid and butter.

- **Always defrost frozen fish before cooking.** To defrost fish: Microwave for 6 to 7 minutes per pound at **DEFROST OR MEDIUM LOW** (30%), turning over once.

- **To cook fish:** Cover with waxed paper and microwave for 4 to 6 minutes per pound at HIGH (100%)—140°F. using a probe.

- If sensitive foods such as cheese, eggs, mushrooms, or mayonnaise are included in a fish recipe, microwave for 8 to 10 minutes per pound at MEDIUM HIGH (70%).

- If snails, clams, or oysters start to "pop," microwave them also at MEDIUM HIGH (70%).

- **Cook fish until it flakes when lifted gently with a fork. DO NOT OVERCOOK, as overcooked fish is firm, dry, and crumbly.** When fish becomes opaque, losing its translucence, it is done.

- **Does your microwave smell fishy?** Microwave 1 slice lemon for 1½ minutes or 2 tablespoons lemon juice in ½ cup water for 2½ minutes at HIGH (100%). The odor will disappear.

TIPS
· · · · ·

You may substitute any cracker crumbs or bread crumbs for the wheat cracker crumbs.

Pour the milk gently over and around the fish so that the coating does not slide off the fish.

· · · · ·

Low in calories.

¼ cup reduced-calorie
   margarine
1 cup wheat cracker
   crumbs

1 pound fish fillets,
   thawed
½ teaspoon seasoned salt
   (optional)
3 tablespoons milk

1. Microwave margarine in a flat 2-quart casserole for 1 minute at HIGH (100%) until melted.

2. Stir in cracker crumbs. Remove half of the crumb mixture.

3. Arrange fish over crumb mixture. Sprinkle fish with salt and remaining cracker crumb mixture. Pour milk over fish. Cover with waxed paper.

4. Microwave for 5 to 7 minutes at HIGH (100%) until fish flakes with a fork. Let stand 2 minutes.

Yields: 4 servings (approximately 220 calories each).

· ❈ ·

Variation: Substitute 1 package fish coating mix (such as Shake 'n Bake) for the cracker crumbs.

SHRIMP CREOLE

— · · · · · —

Low in calories.

1 tablespoon oil or diet margarine
½ cup chopped onion
½ cup chopped celery
¼ cup chopped green pepper
1½ tablespoons cornstarch plus 1 teaspoon sugar or sugar substitute

16-ounce can stewed tomatoes
8-ounce can tomato sauce
½ teaspoon chili powder
½ teaspoon garlic salt
12–16 ounces raw shrimp, shelled and deveined

1. In a 1-quart casserole, combine oil, onion, celery, and green pepper. Cover and microwave for 3 to 4 minutes at HIGH (100%) until vegetables are tender. Stir in cornstarch and sugar.

2. Add remaining ingredients. Cover. Microwave for 5 to 6 minutes at HIGH (100%) or until shrimp is opaque and tender, stirring once or twice during cooking. (Do not overcook or shrimp will become tough.) Let stand 2 minutes. Serve over hot rice if desired.

Yields: 4 servings (approximately 180 calories per serving).

——— · · ———

For calorie watchers: I
have used reduced-cal-
orie mayonnaise success-
fully in the Parmesan
cheese sauce variation.

HALIBUT IN DIET LEMON SAUCE
(OR PARMESAN CHEESE SAUCE)

———— · · · · · ————

· FISH ·

8–12 ounce halibut fillet

· DIET LEMON SAUCE ·

1 tablespoon diet
  margarine
2 tablespoons chopped
  onion
2 teaspoons chopped
  parsley

1 teaspoon lemon juice
¼ teaspoon prepared
  mustard
¼ teaspoon garlic powder
  or garlic salt

1. Place halibut in a 9-inch microwave dish.

2. Combine remaining ingredients for diet lemon sauce in a
1-cup measure. Microwave for 1 minute at HIGH (100%).
Pour lemon sauce over halibut.

3. Cover and microwave for 5 to 7 minues at HIGH
(100%), or until fish is fork tender. Let stand 1 minute.

Yields: 2 to 3 servings (120 calories each).

———— · ❄ · ————

Variation: For Parmesan cheese sauce, combine 2 tablespoons butter, 2 tablespoons mayonnaise, 2 tablespoons
chopped onion, 2 teaspoons lemon juice, and ⅓ cup Parmesan
cheese. Substitute Parmesan cheese sauce for lemon sauce.

SAUCY VEGETABLE FISH FILLETS

· · · · ·

Low in calories.

⅓ cup chopped celery	1 tablespoon cornstarch
⅓ cup chopped onion	dissolved in 1 table-
⅔ cup sliced mushrooms	spoon water
¼ cup water	1 teaspoon dried parsley
1 pound fish fillets (torsk,	for garnish
cod, etc.), thawed if	
frozen	

1. Microwave celery, onion, mushrooms, and water in a flat 2-quart casserole, covered, for 3 to 4 minutes at HIGH (100%).

2. Slip fish under vegetables. Microwave, covered, for 4 to 5 minutes at HIGH (100%) until fish flakes easily with a fork. (Use waxed paper to cover.)

3. Drain fish juices into a custard cup. Stir cornstarch and water into the juices until smooth (except for fish pieces). Microwave for 1 to 2 minutes at HIGH (100%) until thick, stirring once.

4. Pour over fish. Microwave again for 1 to 2 minutes at HIGH (100%). Sprinkle with parsley to garnish.

Yields: 4 servings (100 calories each).

———— · ❄ · ————

Most fish is naturally low in calories. With the added vegetables, this dish makes a tasty but low-calorie entrée.

FISH FILLETS IN CUCUMBER SAUCE

T I P S

The seasoned salt adds a distinct flavor to the sauce but also adds some sodium so it may be omitted if necessary for your diet.

· · · · ·

Low in calories.

· FISH ·

1 pound halibut, cod, perch, or any white fish fillets

1 tablespoon lemon juice

· CUCUMBER SAUCE ·

1 small cucumber, sliced
3 green onions, chopped
⅔ cup plain yogurt
½ teaspoon dill weed

2 teaspoons lemon juice
½ teaspoon seasoned salt (optional)
parsley sprig and lemon slice for garnish

1. Arrange fish in a flat 1½-quart casserole. Sprinkle with lemon juice. Cover with waxed paper. Microwave for 4 to 5 minutes at HIGH (100%) until fish flakes easily with a fork.

2. Puree cucumber sauce ingredients together using a blender or food processor.

3. Microwave sauce for 2 to 3 minutes at MEDIUM (50%) until hot. Pour over cooked fish. Serve garnished with a parsley sprig and lemon slice.

Yields: 3 to 4 servings (109 calories each).

· ❄ ·

ORANGE ROUGHY ALMONDINE

——— · · · · · ———

Lemon juice may be substituted for the lime juice, if desired.

Low in calories.

· FISH ·

1 pound orange roughy
  fillets
1 teaspoon plain gelatin
1½ tablespoons lime juice

½ teaspoon seasoned salt
  (optional)
2 tablespoons snipped
  parsley

· TOASTED ALMONDS ·

¼ cup sliced almonds

2 tablespoons butter or
  reduced-calorie mar-
  garine

1. Place fish fillets in a flat 1½-quart casserole. Sprinkle with gelatin, seasoned salt, parsley, and lime juice. Cover with a casserole lid.

2. Microwave for 4 to 6 minutes at HIGH (100%) until fish flakes easily with a fork. Let stand 5 minutes.

3. Mix almonds and butter in a 9-inch round or square dish. Microwave, uncovered, for 1½ to 3 minutes at HIGH (100%) until toasted, stirring often.

4. Serve fish topped with butter and almonds.

Yields: 3 to 4 servings (220 calories each).

——— · ❄ · ———

MEATS

· · · · ·

- Tender meats such as hamburger, steaks, chops, etc., can be microwaved quickly at HIGH (100%). No covering is needed. However, waxed paper, a paper towel, or napkin may be used to cover tender meats to prevent splattering during microwaving.

- Less tender meats such as roasts, fresh hams, stew meat, round steak, etc., should be microwaved slowly with water added and covered tightly with a lid or plastic wrap. Microwave at HIGH (100%) to heat through and then again at MEDIUM (50%) or DEFROST/MEDIUM LOW (30%) to cook and tenderize.

- Cooked or cured hams, porks, Canadian bacon, etc., should be microwaved at MEDIUM HIGH (70%) to prevent the outer edges from drying out.

- DO NOT use a conventional meat thermometer in the microwave oven. You may insert it when the meat is removed from the oven to quickly check the temperature.

- Always defrost frozen meats before cooking. (Frozen meats should not be defrosted in their original packages.) Always shield thin ends or boney tips of meat with foil to prevent overcooking.

- Always shape meat into a ring or doughnut shape, whenever possible, for even cooking or defrosting.

- Freeze meats in a doughnut shape for even defrosting later.

- Roasts will cook more evenly if turned over twice during microwaving.

- Arrange meat for microwaving with the thickest pieces to the outside.

- Brown meats for main dishes by crumbling into a plastic strainer over a casserole that will cook and drain the grease at once.

- Large cuts of meat require 10 to 15 minutes of standing time, covered tightly. Internal temperature may rise as much as 15°F. during the standing time.

- Small cuts of meat require 5 minutes of standing time, covered.

- Standing time is important for defrosting meats too. If a recipe says to microwave for 5 minutes at DEFROST/MEDIUM LOW (30%) and let stand for 5 minutes, the total defrosting time is 10 minutes (the meat will not be defrosted until after the standing time).

- Meats taste better when microwaved above juices on a rack (or use onion slices or celery ribs to improvise a rack).

- Microwave roasts will never flake off the fork like those cooked for 3 to 4 hours in a conventional oven. They will, however, be tender, firm, and flavorful.

- Microwave tough meats for 20 minutes per pound at DEFROST/MEDIUM LOW (30%) to tenderize.

MEATS: DEFROSTING AND COOKING CHART

To **DEFROST:** Remove packaging and place in a microwave dish.

MEAT	TIME	POWER LEVEL(S)	STANDING TIME
Hamburger, steaks, bacon, chops, stew meats, and other small packages of meat	5–8 minutes per pound	DEFROST (30%)	5 minutes
Roasts, corned beef, ribs, and other large pieces of meat over 2 inches thick	5–6 minutes per pound	MEDIUM (50%)	30 minutes

To **COOK:** Place on a microwave roasting rack or casserole dish. Coat with Micro Shake or browning powder, if desired. For tender meats: Microwave uncovered or covered only with waxed paper. For less tender meats: Cover with plastic wrap or casserole lid.

AMOUNT	TIME	POWER LEVEL(S)	STANDING TIME
HAMBURGERS: per 4- to 5-ounce patty (formed into a flat doughnut shape, placed above juices, covered with paper towel)			
1	2½–3½ minutes	HIGH (100%)	2 minutes
2	5–5½ minutes	same	same
4	6–7 minutes	same	same
STEAKS: rib-eye, sirloin, T-bone, beef, pork, venison, etc.			
per pound	5 minutes	HIGH (100%)	3 minutes
PORK OR LAMB CHOPS: 5-ounce chops (covered with waxed paper)			
1 chop	1 minute and 5 minutes	HIGH (100%) MEDIUM (50%)	3 minutes
ROUND STEAKS: (covered with plastic wrap)			
per pound	5 minutes and 15 minutes	HIGH (100%) MEDIUM (50%)	3 minutes
POT ROASTS: chuck, arm, rump, loin, etc. (placed in a plastic cooking bag)			
per pound	20 minutes	DEFROST (30%)	10 minutes
Standing rib roasts:			
per pound	5 minutes rare—5 minutes medium—6 minutes well—7 minutes	HIGH (100%) and MEDIUM (50%) same same	10 minutes same same

AMOUNT	TIME	POWER LEVEL(S)	STANDING TIME
Cooked ham:			
per pound	10 minutes and 8–10 minutes	HIGH (100%) MEDIUM HIGH (70%)	10 minutes
Stew meat:			
per pound	5–6 minutes and 15 minutes	HIGH (100%) MEDIUM (50%)	5 minutes

Stew meat and vegetables: Microwave uncooked meat (5 minutes per pound) at HIGH (100%) first to cook, then add the vegetables and microwave at MEDIUM (50%) until tender.

Bacon: Place on rack or paper towels (3). Cover with paper towels (2).

per slice	30–60 seconds	HIGH (100%)	2 minutes

Hot Dogs: Place hot dog in bun. (Wrap in a paper towel to prevent a soggy bun.) Microwave at MEDIUM HIGH (70%) for 40–50 seconds each. Without bun, place on a bacon rack or plate. Microwave 25–30 seconds each at MEDIUM HIGH (70%). Do NOT spread hot dogs or buns with condiments before microwaving and do NOT microwave more than 4 hot dogs at a time.

CORNED BEEF AND CABBAGE

— · · · · · —

A great New England boiled dinner.

2–2½ pounds corned beef
  brisket (with
  seasonings)
1 cup water
4 carrots, peeled and
  sliced ½ inch thick

2 large potatoes, peeled
  and cut into chunks
1 cabbage, cut into
  wedges
1 large onion, cut into
  chunks

1. Place corned beef and the seasonings that come with it in a 2- or 3-quart casserole. Add water. Cover.

2. Microwave for 10 to 12 minutes at HIGH (100%).

3. Microwave again for 25 minutes at MEDIUM (50%). Turn meat over and add remaining ingredients.

4. Cover and microwave again for 30 to 45 minutes at MEDIUM (50%) or until meat is tender. Let stand 10 minutes.

Yields: 4 to 6 servings.

— · ❄ · —

TIPS
· · · · ·

Although this dinner takes more than an hour in the microwave oven, it still saves time over the conventional oven method.

You will always find suc-
cess with meatloaf when it
is shaped in a ring and microwaved at MEDIUM
HIGH (70%).

The browning powder is
optional as the Saucy Topping helps enhance the
appearance.

BEST MICROWAVE MEAT LOAF WITH SAUCY TOPPING

——— · · · · · ———

*Ready to eat in 20 minutes and tasty enough
for company.*

· MEAT LOAF ·

1¼–1½ pounds lean
   ground beef
1 egg, beaten
¾ cup dried bread crumbs
   or cracker crumbs, or ½
   cup dry oatmeal

⅓ cup ketchup
1 package dry onion soup
   mix, dissolved in ¼ cup
   water
Micro Shake, or browning
   powder (optional)

· SAUCY TOPPING ·

¼ cup ketchup
2 tablespoons brown
   sugar

¼ teaspoon nutmeg
1 teaspoon dry mustard

1. Combine all ingredients except topping. Shape into a ring. Sprinkle with Micro Shake for browning.

2. Cover with waxed paper or a paper towel. Microwave for 15 minutes at MEDIUM HIGH (70%).

3. Combine topping ingredients. Pour ¾ of saucy topping on meat loaf. Microwave again for 5 to 7 minutes at MEDIUM HIGH (70%). Drizzle with remaining topping. Let stand 5 minutes.

Yields: 4 to 6 servings.

——— · · ———

MEAT LOAF FOR ONE OR TWO
(IN A MUG)

—————— · · · · · ——————

¼ pound ground beef
2 tablespoons bread
   crumbs or dry oatmeal
1 tablespoon ketchup

1 teaspoon milk
2 teaspoons onion soup
   mix
Micro Shake (optional)

1. Combine all ingredients. Pat into a microwave-safe mug or custard cup. Make a small hole in the center. Sprinkle with Micro Shake if desired.

2. Microwave for 3 to 4 minutes at HIGH (100%). Let stand 3 minutes.

For two: Double the ingredients. Place in 2 mugs. Microwave for 6 to 7 minutes at HIGH (100%).

Variation: Serve topped with 1 tablespoon ketchup, mixed with 1 teaspoon brown sugar and a dash of dry mustard. (This is enough for two mugs.)

—————— · ❄ · ——————

SLOPPY JOES

—————— · · · · · ——————

Quick and easy.

1–1½ pounds ground
   beef, crumbled
½ onion, chopped
1 teaspoon chili seasoning

dash of salt, pepper, and
   sugar
2 tablespoons ketchup
10½-ounce can tomato
   soup
6–8 hamburger buns

1. Microwave beef and onion in a covered casserole for 5 to 6 minutes at HIGH (100%) until meat is no longer pink. Drain grease. Add seasonings and ketchup, mixing well.

TIPS
· · · · ·

For calorie watchers: Lean ground beef or ground turkey may be substituted for the ground beef.

I usually use William's Chili Seasoning, but you may use any taco or chili seasoning, to taste.

2. Stir in tomato soup. Cover with paper towel. Microwave for 5 to 6 minutes at HIGH (100%), stirring twice. Let stand 5 minutes. Serve in hamburger buns.

Yields: 6 to 8 servings.

———— · ❄ · ————

 POLISH SAUSAGE
———— · · · · · ————

You may use this recipe for any smoked or cooked sausages.

1–1½ pounds Polish sausage (fully cooked), slashed every 1 or 2 inches
1 onion, sliced

12-ounce can beer
dash of pepper
1 tablespoon prepared mustard

1. Combine all ingredients in a 2-quart casserole. Cover with a casserole lid.
2. Microwave for 9 to 11 minutes at HIGH (100%) or until hot (165°F.).
3. Slice sausage and serve with mustard or other condiments.

Yields: 4 to 6 servings.

———— · ❄ · ————

SWEDISH MEATBALLS

———— · · · · · ————

2 eggs

⅔ cup milk

½ cup cracker or bread
crumbs

½ teaspoon salt

⅛ teaspoon cloves

⅛ teaspoon nutmeg

⅛ teaspoon allspice

2 teaspoons brown sugar

½ cup chopped onion

2 tablespoons butter

1¼ pound ground beef
(half may be ground
pork)

Micro Shake (optional)

10 ¾-ounce can cream of
mushroom soup

1 tablespoon instant beef
bouillon, dissolved in 1
cup water

1 cup sour cream

TIPS
· · · · ·
This seems like a lot of ingredients but half of the list
is common household
spices or seasonings.

1. Mix eggs, milk, and cracker crumbs in a mixing bowl.

2. Stir in spices and brown sugar.

3. Microwave onion in the butter for 2½ minutes at HIGH
(100%) in a 2-quart casserole.

4. Stir into the egg and spice mixture. Mix in the beef.

5. Shape into twelve 1½-inch meatballs and place in a 2- or
3-quart casserole. Sprinkle with Micro Shake to coat for
browning (optional). Cover with waxed paper.

*6. Microwave for 8 to 10 minutes at HIGH (100%), stir-
ring twice. Drain.

7. Add soup and bouillon water. Cover with lid or plastic
wrap.

*8. Microwave for 10 to 12 minutes at MEDIUM (50%).

9. Add sour cream, stir, and serve.

Yields: 4 servings.

———— · ❈ · ————

Compacts: Microwave for 8 to 10 minutes at HIGH
(100%) instead of step #8.

· ·
*Rotate casserole while microwaving, if necessary, for even cooking.

ITALIAN MEATBALLS

· · · · ·

Any grated cheese works well. I usually use cheddar or Parmesan cheese.

I like to use Ragu Natural spaghetti sauce in the sauce.

A great accompaniment to any pasta!

· MEATBALLS ·

1 pound lean ground beef
½ cup cracker crumbs
⅓ cup grated Parmesan
  cheese

½ teaspoon Italian
  seasoning
½ teaspoon garlic salt
1 tablespoon dried parsley
1 egg

· SAUCE ·

16-ounce jar spaghetti
  sauce
dash of sugar or sugar
  substitute
1 tablespoon wine,
  cooking sherry, or water

½ teaspoon Italian
  seasoning
½ cup grated cheese

1. Combine all ingredients for the meatballs. Shape into 12 to 15 1-inch meatballs. Microwave on a bacon rack or in a 2-quart casserole, covered with waxed paper, for 7 to 8 minutes at HIGH (100%). Drain off fat.

2. Combine spaghetti sauce, sugar, wine, and seasoning in a 2-quart casserole.

3. Add meatballs. Cover.

4. Microwave for 10 to 12 minutes at MEDIUM HIGH (70%). Let stand 5 minutes. Serve with your favorite pasta topped with grated cheese.

Yields: 4 servings.

———— · ❄ · ————

Variation: For Italian meat sauce, substitute 1 pound lean hamburger that has been crumbled and browned. Omit step #1. Add browned, drained hamburger to the sauce in step #3.

ROLLED RUMP ROAST

———— · · · · · ————

The bacon adds a stove-top browning effect.

3- to 5-pound rolled rump
  roast
Micro Shake or Natural
  browning powder
  (optional)

2 tablespoons dry onion
  soup mix
6 uncooked bacon strips
1 tablespoon water

1. Sprinkle roast with Micro Shake and onion soup mix.
2. Cover roast with bacon strips secured with toothpicks.
3. Place roast in a 2-quart casserole. Add water. Cover with a casserole lid.
4. Microwave for 20 minutes per pound at DEFROST/ LOW (30%). Turn over 3 to 4 times during microwaving.
5. Let stand 10 to 20 minutes.

Yields: 6 to 10 servings.

———— · ❄ · ————

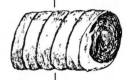

· ·

Marriage is an institution, held together by two books; cook and check.

This dinner may also be microwaved in a plastic cooking bag, which will give very tender results. Place the food in a bag first and then into the casserole. Close the bag with a plastic tie, string, or dental floss, leaving an opening ½ inch in diameter. Follow the directions as listed (but do NOT cover with a lid).

POT ROAST DINNER

· · · · ·

2- to 3-pound chuck (or pot) roast
Micro Shake (optional)
1 package dry onion soup mix
¼ cup water

4 carrots, cut into sticks
3 potatoes, cut into wedges
1½ tablespoons cornstarch, dissolved completely in ¼ cup water

1. Pierce both sides of meat several times with a fork, and then sprinkle liberally with Micro Shake (optional).

2. Place roast in a 2-quart casserole. Sprinkle with soup mix. Add water.

*3. Cover tightly and microwave for 30 minutes at MEDIUM (50%). Turn roast over. Add vegetables.

*4. Re-cover. Microwave for 40 to 50 minutes at DEFROST (30%), or until meat and vegetables are fork tender. (Turn meat over once or twice again for even cooking results.)

5. Remove meat and vegetables.

6. Stir dissolved cornstarch into dripping to make gravy. Stir well.

7. Microwave for 2 to 3 minutes at HIGH (100%) until thick. Stir well.

8. Serve the beef sliced thinly across the grain and drizzled with gravy.

Yields: 4 to 6 servings.

———— · ❈ · ————

*Rotate dish twice, if necessary, for even cooking.

SAVORY POT ROAST AND GRAVY

2- to 4-pound pot roast
(cross cut rib chuck
roast works well)
Micro Shake for meat
(optional)
3 tablespoons water

½ (10¾ ounce) can cream
of mushroom soup (use
full can if more gravy is
desired)
1 envelope onion soup mix
1 tablespoon
Worcestershire sauce

This roast may also be microwaved in a plastic
cooking bag for very
tender results. Place the
food in a plastic cooking
bag first and then into the
casserole. Close the bag
with a plastic tie, string, or
dental floss, leaving an
opening ½ inch in diame-
ter. Follow the directions
as listed (only do NOT
cover with a lid).

1. Sprinkle Micro Shake on both sides of roast.

2. Combine remaining ingredients and pour over roast in a 2-quart casserole.

3. Cover tightly. Microwave for 20 minutes per pound at MEDIUM LOW (70%), turning over twice for most even cooking. Let stand 5 to 10 minutes. Slice into ¼-inch slices across the grain.

Yields: 6 to 8 servings.

STUFFED GREEN PEPPERS

A lovely luncheon idea and not too high in calories.

6 medium green peppers
⅓ cup chopped onion
1 pound ground beef
¾ cup tomato soup or
tomato sauce
1 egg
1 teaspoon seasoned salt

1 tablespoon Worcester-
shire sauce
½ cup bread crumbs or ¼
cup Minute Rice
½ cup cottage cheese
1 cup shredded American
or mozzarella cheese

1. Prepare peppers by washing, then removing tops, cores, and seeds. Arrange in a large flat (12x8-inch) casserole. Micro-wave, covered, for 2 to 3 minutes at HIGH (100%). Let stand 5 minutes.

2. Combine remaining ingredients, except shredded cheese, in a mixing bowl until well mixed.

3. Spoon meat mixture into peppers. Cover lightly with waxed paper.

4. Microwave for 15 to 19 minutes at HIGH (100%) until meat is well done.

5. Top with shredded cheese and let stand 5 minutes.

Yields: 6 servings.

———— · ❄ · ————

Compacts: Microwave for 20 to 25 minutes at HIGH (100%) in step #4.

PEPPER STEAK

———— · · · · · ————

1½ pounds beef flank steak	16-ounce can whole tomatoes
¼ cup flour	8-ounce can tomato sauce
3 tablespoons onion soup mix	2 teaspoons soy sauce (optional)
1 green pepper, cut into strips	2 teaspoons chopped chives or parsley

1. Slice steak diagonally into ¼ inch strips. Place strips in a 2-quart casserole. Add flour and soup mix, tossing to coat meat.

2. Combine remaining ingredients with tomatoes. Pour over all.

3. Cover tightly. Microwave for 15 to 20 minutes at MEDIUM HIGH (70%) or until beef strips are tender. Stir. Let stand 10 minutes. Serve over rice.

Yields: 4 to 6 servings.

———— · ❄ · ————

Compacts: Microwave in step #3 for 15 to 20 minutes at HIGH (100%).

TIPS
· · · ·

One to 1½ pounds boneless top round steak, pounded to ¼ inch thick, may be substituted for the beef flank steak.

One 16-ounce can stewed tomatoes may be substituted for the whole tomatoes.

BEEF STROGANOFF

———— · · · · · ————

1 to 1½ pounds beef top
   round or sirloin steak
   (cut into thin 2-inch-
   long slices)
Micro Shake or browning
   powder (optional)
1 onion, sliced ¼ inch
   thick
¼ teaspoon garlic salt

4½-ounce jar button
   mushrooms
1¼ cups beef bouillon
¼ cup red wine, cooking
   sherry, or water
2 tablespoons cornstarch
1 cup sour cream or
   yogurt or cottage
   cheese, blender smooth
hot buttered noodles

1. Coat meat with Micro Shake (if desired). Add onion and garlic salt. Microwave, covered, in a 3-quart casserole for 7 to 8 minutes on HIGH (100%).

2. Stir in mushrooms with juice, and beef bouillon.

3. Mix wine and cornstarch in a small bowl until smooth. Stir into broth. Cover.

4. Microwave for 20 to 25 minutes at MEDIUM (50%) or until fork tender. Very tough meat turns out best when micro-waved for 30 to 35 minutes at DEFROST (30%).

5. Stir in sour cream and microwave again, covered, for 3 to 4 minutes at MEDIUM HIGH (70%). Let stand 5 minutes.

6. Serve over hot buttered noodles.

Yields: 4 to 6 servings.

———— · · ————

TIPS
· · · · ·

The size of the onion may be varied according to your liking.

  For beef bouillon: You may use canned beef broth or 2 cubes beef bouillon dissolved in 1¼ cups hot water.

TIPS
· · · · ·

For bottom round steak: Use DEFROST (30%) in step #3.

For top round steak: Use MEDIUM (50%) in step #3.

· · · · ·

1 pound round steak
Micro Shake or browning
  powder, for meat
  (optional)
2 tablespoons flour
¼ teaspoon onion powder
¼ teaspoon garlic powder
  (optional)
2 teaspoons oil

1 large onion, sliced
1 cup natural spaghetti
  sauce (like Ragu)
2 tablespoons wine or
  cooking sherry
  (optional)
dash of sugar or sugar
  substitute

1. Coat round steak with Micro Shake and then sprinkle with flour, seasonings, and oil on both sides. Place on a thick onion slice in a 2-quart casserole. Microwave for 5 to 6 minutes at HIGH (100%).

2. Top with sliced onions and cover with spaghetti sauce, sherry, and sugar.

3. Cover with lid or plastic wrap and microwave for 30 to 35 minutes at MEDIUM (50%) or DEFROST (30%) or until fork tender. Let stand 5 minutes.

Yields: 4 to 6 servings.

· ❄ ·

CHINESE BEEF AND PEA PODS

· · · · ·

TIPS
· · · ·

One 8-ounce can sliced and drained water chestnuts may be substituted for the mushrooms.

1–1½ pounds top round or sirloin steak
Micro Shake for meat
¼ cup soy sauce
1 tablespoon red wine or water
1 tablespoon brown sugar
¼ teaspoon ginger
2 tablespoons cornstarch, dissolved in 2 tablespoons water

6-ounce can sliced mushrooms, drained
6-ounce package pea pods, thawed
1 cup bean sprouts, drained (optional)
¼ cup sliced green onions (about 3)
3 cups cooked rice (optional)

1. Trim fat from beef. Cut into 2-inch-long strips (¼ inch thick). Sprinkle meat liberally with Micro Shake. Mix soy sauce, wine, brown sugar, and ginger. Pour over steak in a 1½-quart casserole. Cover. Microwave for 5 to 7 minutes at MEDIUM HIGH (70%), stirring once, or until meat is no longer pink.

2. Drain juices into a small bowl. Add cornstarch and water. Stir until smooth. Microwave for 1 to 2 minutes at HIGH (100%) until boiling.

3. Stir thickened juices into meat. Add mushrooms, pea pods, sprouts, if desired, and onions. Microwave for 7 to 8 minutes at MEDIUM HIGH (70%) or until steaming hot and meat is fork tender, stirring once. Serve over cooked rice.

Yields: 4 to 6 servings.

· ❄ ·

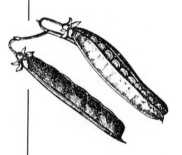

This entrée actually improves in flavor when reheated the next day.

———— · · · · · ————

An easy one-dish microwave oven meal.

1 cup tomato juice
1 tablespoon cornstarch
low-calorie sugar substitute (or fructose) equal to 3 teaspoons sugar (1½ packets)
1 teaspoon beef bouillon granules
¼ teaspoon pepper
1 teaspoon salt (optional

1 pound boneless round steak, thinly sliced into strips and coated with 1 teaspoon bouquet sauce or Micro Shake to increase browning (optional)
2 small white potatoes, peeled and thinly sliced
4 carrots, thinly sliced
2 ribs celery, thinly sliced
1 onion, thinly sliced and separated into rings
1 tomato, chopped (optional)

1. In a 3-quart casserole, blend tomato juice, cornstarch, sugar substitute, beef bouillon, pepper, and salt. Add steak strips, stirring to coat. Stir in remaining vegetables, except for the tomato. Cover with a casserole lid.

2. Microwave at HIGH (100%) for 5 minutes. Stir.

3. Microwave at MEDIUM (50%) for 30 to 40 minutes or until meat and vegetables are fork tender. Stir in the tomato the last 5 minutes. Let stand (covered) 5 minutes before serving.

Yields: 4 to 6 servings (230 calories per serving).

———— · · ————

COMPANY ROUND STEAK

— · · · · · —

1½ pounds round steak, cut into serving pieces
¼ cup flour
Micro Shake or browning powder (optional)
1 onion, sliced and separated into rings

3 tablespoons dry onion soup mix
1 tablespoon Worcestershire sauce
1 teaspoon chopped parsley plus parsley for granish
10¾-ounce can cream of mushroom soup

1. Pound or score steak pieces. Dredge in flour and sprinkle with Micro Shake.

2. Combine remaining ingredients in a 1-quart casserole. Place steak pieces in the casserole and blend. Cover tightly with casserole lid.

3. Microwave for 8 minutes at HIGH (100%). Stir. Re-cover and microwave again for 30 to 40 minutes at MEDIUM (50%) or until meat is fork tender. Let stand 5 minutes. Serve garnished or sprinkled with parsley.

Yields: 4 to 6 servings.

— · ❋ · —

EASY PORK CHOP AND RICE CASSEROLE

TIPS

The appearance of pork chops is helped by coating them with browning powder. Without the browning powder, microwaved pork chops appear a bit gray.

1–1¼ pounds thin pork chops (5–6)
Micro Shake or Natural browning powder (optional)
2 onions, sliced

1 cup uncooked instant rice
1 cup spaghetti sauce (natural), nongeneric
2 tablespoons water

· TOPPING ·

2 tablespoons Parmesan cheese

¾ cup grated mozzarella cheese

*1. Coat pork chops with Micro Shake. Place in a 2-quart flat casserole. Top with onion slices. Cover. Microwave for 6 to 7 minutes at HIGH (100%).

*2. Mix remaining ingredients, except topping. Pour over chops. Cover. Microwave for 6 to 7 minutes at HIGH (100%). Microwave again for 12 to 15 minutes at MEDIUM (50%).

3. Sprinkle with topping immediately. (Topping may be omitted). Let stand (covered) until cheese melts.

Yields: 4 to 6 servings.

——— · ❄ · ———

Compacts: Microwave for 6 minutes in step #1. Add spaghetti sauce mixture. Microwave for 6 minutes at HIGH (100%) in step #2. Let stand 6 minutes. Microwave again for 6 minutes at HIGH (100%) until tender.

. . . .
*Rotate dish after every microwaving time, if necessary, for even cooking.

· · 171 · ·

SPECIAL PORK CHOPS
SERVED OVER RICE

. . . . .

⅓ cup raisins

⅓ cup brown sugar

1 onion, sliced

1 cup uncooked rice
(wild, brown, white, or
mixed), not instant

1 cup apple cider or juice

dash of nutmeg

½ cup water

5–6 pork chops (1½–2
pounds), coated with
Micro Shake or
browning sauce
(optional)

1. Microwave all of the ingredients, except coated pork chops, in a 3-quart covered casserole for 6 to 8 minutes at HIGH (100%) until boiling.

* 2. Place coated chops over rice. Cover. Microwave for 40 to 50 minutes at DEFROST (30%) until chops are done. Let stand 5 minutes.

Yields: 5 to 6 servings.

* Rotate casserole twice, if necessary, for even cooking.

TIPS

· · · · ·

Arrange pork chops in the casserole with bony parts toward the center for even cooking.

You may use a casserole lid or plastic wrap (with a vented edge) to cover the casserole.

SWEET-AND-SOUR PORK

. . . . .

Cut pork into ¾-inch cubes for best results.

Cubed pork may be cooked at a higher power level than pork chops.

1½ pounds cubed pork
  tenderloin
2½ tablespoons
  cornstarch
2 tablespoons soy sauce
3 tablespoons brown
  sugar
3 tablespoons vinegar

½ tablespoon salt
¼ teaspoon ginger
13-ounce can pineapple
  chunks and juice
1 onion, sliced and
  separated
1 green pepper, cut into
  strips

1. Mix pork and cornstarch together in a 2-quart casserole.

2. Stir in remaining ingredients, except green pepper. Cover with casserole lid.

3. Microwave for 15 minutes at MEDIUM HIGH (70%). Stir in green pepper. Re-cover. Microwave again for 10 to 15 minutes at MEDIUM HIGH (70%). Let stand 5 minutes.

Yields: 4 to 6 servings.

——— · ❄ · ———

HAM WITH CHERRY OR PLUM GLAZE

— · · · · · —

3-pound boneless, cooked
  ham

· CHERRY GLAZE ·

1 21-ounce can cherry pie   1 tablespoon lemon juice
  filling   ¼ teaspoon cloves

· PLUM GLAZE ·

16-ounce can plums   ¼ teaspoon cloves
¼ cup brown sugar

1. Combine ingredients for glaze of your choice. Set aside.
2. Place ham, fat side down, on a roasting rack. Cover loosely with plastic wrap. Microwave for 10 minutes at HIGH (100%).
3. Turn ham over. Cover again. Microwave for 20 minutes at MEDIUM HIGH (70%). Spread with half of glaze. Continue to microwave for 5 to 10 minutes at MEDIUM HIGH (70%) or until internal temperature reaches 130°F. on a probe or microwave meat thermometer.
4. Top with remaining glaze. Cover with aluminum foil and let stand 10 minutes.

Yields: 8 to 12 servings.

— · ❊ · —

Compacts: Microwave at HIGH (100%) instead of MEDIUM HIGH (70%) in step #3.

. . . .

The grass is greener on the other side of the fence, but it is just as hard to mow.

The Cherry Glaze is perfect for holiday entertaining. It is the easiest and yet tastiest way to cook ham that I have ever tried.

If you are using a probe, insert it into the center of the ham after spreading the glaze on it in step #3. Program for 130°F. at MEDIUM HIGH (70%).

If top edge of ham begins to overcook, shield it with a 1½-inch strip of foil (see pages 9 and 10 for tips on shielding).

Use your convection microwave or your microwave plus your regular oven.

Be sure to use a casserole and lid that is both microwave- and oven-safe (like Pyrex or Corning Ware).

Three convection microwave settings are suggested. Choose the one that corresponds to the power setting on your convection microwave oven.

PORK CHOP CASSEROLE

———— · · · · · ————

6 pork chops (1½ pounds)	¾ cup uncooked rice
Micro Shake or browning powder (optional)	31-ounce can tomatoes plus juice
2 large sliced onions	1 teaspoon seasoned salt

1. Coat pork chops with Micro Shake. Microwave, covered, in a 2-quart casserole for 6 minutes at HIGH (100%). Remove from casserole.

2. Place half of onions, rice, and tomatoes in the casserole. Arrange chops in a single layer over rice. Add remaining onion, rice, and tomatoes. Sprinkle with seasoned salt. Cover with a glass casserole lid.

3. For Convection Microwave: Low-Mix Bake at 350°F. OR Combination #2 OR Code #2 for 45 minutes. Let stand for 5 minutes.

For Microwave and a regular oven: Bake for 40 minutes in a regular oven at 350°F.; transfer to your microwave and microwave for 10 minutes at MEDIUM (50%).

Yields: 4 to 6 servings.

———— · ❄ · ————

POULTRY

· · · · ·

- **Choose poultry, when possible, that is NOT in-jected with a butter solution.** The bird will micro-wave better without the fat and you will save calories.

- **Remove "pop-out" temperature doneness indica-tors.** They do not work in a microwave.

- **Do not use a conventional meat thermometer—** it will break. You may insert it quickly when the meat is removed from the oven to check the tem-perature (180°F. in the breast of poultry = DONE).

- **Always defrost poultry completely before cook-ing. To DEFROST POULTRY:** Microwave for 4 minutes per pound at DEFROST (30%). Let stand at least 1 hour before cooking. Over 12 to 14 pounds: Let stand 1½ to 2 hours. (Turn bird over during defrosting.)

- **Use a microwave roasting rack** when cooking whole birds OR place the bird on thick onion slices OR celery ribs to raise it out of its juices.

- **TO COOK POULTRY:** Microwave whole turkey, turkey breasts, and chicken for 5 to 10 minutes at HIGH (100%) to start the bird cooking and then for 7 to 9 minutes per pound at MEDIUM HIGH (70%) to cook evenly. Turn over during cooking. Let stand, covered, 15 minutes to complete cooking.

· **TO COOK SINGLE PIECES OF CHICKEN:** Microwave ½ breast or 2 legs for 1 minute at HIGH (100%) and again for 5 minutes at MEDIUM HIGH (70%), covered with waxed paper. Let stand 5 minutes.

· **TO COOK A STEWING CHICKEN:** Microwave chicken for 3 to 4 minutes at HIGH (100%) to start cooking and again for 10 minutes per pound at MEDIUM (50%) to tenderize. Stand 5 minutes.

· **TO COOK DUCKLING, PHEASANT, GOOSE, OR CAPON:** Microwave bird for 8 to 9 minutes per pound at MEDIUM HIGH (70%). DO NOT start cooking at HIGH as with other poultry. Drain fat during microwaving. Stand 5 minutes.

· **Shield wings and drumsticks with foil** for half the cooking time to prevent them from drying out when microwaving a whole bird.

· **For outdoor grilling:** Precook poultry pieces by microwaving 2½ to 3 pounds for 15 minutes at MEDIUM HIGH (70%). Then grill chicken for 20 to 25 minutes, basting with bottled barbeque sauce.

This is my favorite low-calorie way to make chicken. The unflavored gelatin gives the chicken a saucy texture.

——— · · · · · ———

Low in calories.

2 tablespoons dried parsley	½ teaspoon onion powder
2 tablespoons dried chives	½ teaspoon salt (optional)
8 ounces fresh mushrooms, sliced	½ teaspoon poultry seasoning
2 small chicken breasts (5–6 ounces each), skinned	1½ teaspoons unflavored gelatin granules (½ package)
⅓ cup lemon juice	1 teaspoon paprika

1. Mix parsley, chives, and mushrooms in a 1-quart casserole.

2. Place chicken on mushrooms. Pour lemon juice over chicken.

3. Sprinkle remaining ingredients over chicken in order given.

4. Cover. Microwave at MEDIUM HIGH (70%) for 11 to 14 minutes or until tender. Let stand 3 minutes before serving.

Yields: 2 servings (approximately 160 calories per serving.)

——— ·  · ———

COMPANY CHICKEN BREASTS

· · · · ·

Very elegant, very good!

2½ ounces sliced chipped beef (optional)	½ (10¾-ounce) can cream of chicken soup
1½ pounds (about 6) boneless chicken breasts	3 ounces cream cheese, soft
Micro Shake for chicken (optional) or paprika	½ cup sour cream
3 strips bacon	1 tablespoon chives (or use sour cream with chives)

1. Cover the bottom of a 2-quart casserole with chipped beef. Place chicken breasts on top of beef. Sprinkle with Micro Shake if desired.

2. Cut bacon strips in half and lay ½ strip on top of each breast. Cover.

3. Microwave for 15 minutes at MEDIUM HIGH (70%).

4. Combine soup, cream cheese, sour cream, and chives. Pour over the chicken breasts.

5. Sprinkle with Micro Shake. Cover.

6. Microwave for 10 to 12 minutes at MEDIUM (50%) or until chicken is fork tender. Let stand 5 minutes. Serve with white or wild rice.

Yields: 6 servings.

———— · ❄ · ————

Compacts: Microwave chicken at HIGH (100%) instead of MEDIUM HIGH (70%) or MEDIUM (50%).

You may substitute cream of mushroom soup for the cream of chicken soup.

One teaspoon of crushed rosemary and one teaspoon of dried parsley may be substituted for the chives.

WHOLE ROASTED CHICKEN
(STUFFED WITH CELERY AND ONION)

——— . . . . . ———

Low in calories.

3- to 4-pound whole frying or roasting chicken	2 tablespoons soft or liquid margarine, butter, or oil
1 small onion, chopped (or add ½ minced garlic)	poultry seasoning paprika
2 stalks celery, chopped	Micro Shake for chicken (optional)

1. Mix onion and celery and place in chicken cavity. Tie chicken legs together with string and fasten wings to body with toothpicks.

2. Place chicken on a roasting rack. Brush with margarine or oil. Sprinkle well with seasonings. Shield wings and bony parts with foil. Cover loosely with waxed paper or plastic wrap.

3. Microwave for 3 minutes at HIGH (100%).

4. Microwave again for 9 minutes per pound at MEDIUM HIGH (70%). Let stand 5 minutes. (If chicken is very meaty and full, microwave breast side down for 4 minutes per pound. Turn over. Microwave breast side up for 5 minutes per pound.) Let stand 5 minutes.

Yields: 4 to 6 servings.

——— · ❄ · ———

Compacts: Follow the same directions using 8 minutes per pound at HIGH (100%) in step #4.

Variation: For breaded stuffing, mix 2 to 3 pieces of bread (cubed) or ½ cup croutons with onions and celery in step #1. Proceed with directions as listed.

OVEN-FRIED CHICKEN
(WITH 11 COATING AND DIP VARIATIONS)

————— · · · · · —————

1 cup coating of choice
  (see below) or 1 package
  prepared coating mix
1 teaspoon paprika and/or
Micro Shake or
browning powder

dip of choice (see below)
2½- to 3-pound broiler
  fryer, cut up

1. Mix coating and paprika. Coat chicken pieces in the dip and the coating mixture. Place coated chicken on a paper plate, towel-lined tray or turntable, or baking rack with the meatiest portions toward the outside. Cover lightly with waxed paper.

*2. Microwave for 18 to 25 minutes at MEDIUM HIGH (70%).

Yields: 4 to 6 servings.

————— · ❄ · —————

Compacts: Microwave for 20 to 25 minutes at HIGH (100%) instead of step #2.

· ·
* Rotate twice, if necessary, for even cooking.

COATINGS (CHOOSE ONE)

· CORNFLAKES COATING ·

2 cups cornflakes,
  crushed
3 tablespoons Parmesan
  cheese

½ teaspoon seasoned salt
1 teaspoon paprika

TIPS
· · · · ·
Shake 'n Bake works well, in regular or barbeque flavors, as a prepared coating mix.

· FLAKY COATING ·

⅓ cup potato flakes   1 teaspoon parsley flakes
⅓ cup bread crumbs   ½ teaspoon garlic salt

· ONION COATING ·

one 6-ounce can fried
    onion rings, crushed

· CORNMEAL COATING ·

½ cup cornmeal   1 teaspoon poppy seed

· STUFFING CRUMB COATING ·

1 cup crushed herb-   ¼ teaspoon salt
    seasoned stuffing   ½ teaspoon basil

· PREPARED (MIX) BARBECUE COATING ·

(Rinse chicken before
    coating. Do not dry; do
    not dip. Coat only.)

· CRACKER COATING ·

1⅓ cups crushed crackers   1 envelope gravy mix
    (Ritz, etc.)   (dry)

DIPS (CHOOSE ONE)

· EGG DIP ·

1 egg
2 tablespoons milk

· RICH DIP ·

1 egg   3 tablespoons melted
1 tablespoon milk   butter

· BUTTER DIP ·

⅓ cup melted butter

· MILK DIP ·

⅓ cup milk

CHICKEN BREASTS PARMESAN OR CHICKEN CORDON BLEU

Serve as a quick company dinner with wild rice.

1 cup dry bread crumbs
½ cup grated Parmesan
    cheese
½ teaspoon garlic salt or
    powder
dash of salt and pepper

1 tablespoon parsley
1 teaspoon paprika
¼ cup melted butter or
    margarine
4 chicken breast halves,
    skinned

1. Combine dry ingredients in a plastic bag.
2. Dip chicken breasts in butter and then shake in bag to coat evenly.
3. Arrange chicken in a shallow baking dish with the thicker pieces toward the outside.
4. Sprinkle remaining crumbs and butter over top of chicken.
5. Microwave for 4 minutes at HIGH (100%) and 12 to 16 minutes at MEDIUM HIGH (70%). For 2 breast halves, cut recipe in half. Microwave for 2 minutes at HIGH (100%) and 9 to 10 minutes at MEDIUM HIGH (70%). Let stand 5 minutes.

Yields 3 to 4 servings.

· ❄ ·

Compacts: Microwave chicken for 15 to 18 minutes at HIGH (100%) instead of step #5.

Variation: Chicken Cordon Bleu, microwave style: Debone chicken breasts. Pound chicken breasts flat. Put ½ slice Swiss cheese and ½ slice cooked ham on chicken. Roll up and proceed with step #1, etc., as directed above.

Skinned poultry pieces have the best appearance after microwaving. Skinning saves calories, too.

Milk may be substituted for the butter.

To melt butter: Microwave ¼ cup in a custard cup for 20 to 30 seconds at HIGH (100%).

Four chicken breast halves should weigh about 2½ to 3 pounds.

Ragu Garden Style spaghetti sauce works well.

CHICKEN CACCIATORE

——— . . . . . ———

Easy and delicious.

2½- to 3-pound frying
   chicken, cut up
16-ounce jar chunky style
   spaghetti sauce

½ package chicken
   coating mix (such as
   Shake 'n Bake) or ⅓ cup
   seasoned dry bread
   crumbs
Micro Shake for chicken
   or browning powder
   (optional)

1. Coat rinsed chicken with crumbs or coating mix and Micro Shake (optional).

2. Arrange chicken, bony side up and meatiest portions to the outside, in a 3-quart or 8x12-inch casserole dish.

*3. Cover tightly. Microwave for 10 minutes at HIGH (100%). Turn chicken over. Top with spaghetti sauce. Cover. Microwave again for 15 to 20 minutes at MEDIUM HIGH (70%). Let stand 5 minutes. Serve with rice, if desired.

Yields: 4 to 6 servings.

——— · ❄ · ———

Compacts: Microwave for 18 to 20 minutes at HIGH (100%) in step #3 instead of the 15 to 20 minutes at MEDIUM HIGH as listed.

Variation: For cacciatore sauce using plain spaghetti sauce, mix one 16-ounce jar spaghetti sauce with 1 teaspoon oregano, dash of sweetener, and 1 (each) tomato, onion, and garlic—all diced. (Substitute for chunky garden style sauce.)

. . . .
*Rotate dish once during cooking, if necessary, for even cooking.

SAVORY CHICKEN AND DRESSING
(OR CORNISH HEN)

_____ · · · · · _____

An easy yet elegant dinner idea.

TIPS
· · · ·
Arrange meatier areas of
the chicken breasts toward
the outside of the casse-
role dish for even cooking.

6-ounce box savory
   stuffing mix
4-ounce can mushrooms
1⅓ cups water or as box
   directions indicate
¼ cup butter or margarine

4 chicken breast halves
   (2½ pounds), skinned
Micro Shake for chicken
   or browning powder
½ teaspoon poultry
   seasoning
½ teaspoon paprika

1. Combine stuffing mix, mushrooms and juice, and water in a 2-quart casserole.

2. Arrange chicken breasts over stuffing.

3. Microwave butter in a small dish for 30 seconds at HIGH (100%) until melted. Pour over chicken.

4. Sprinkle chicken with Micro Shake and poultry seasoning. Cover with waxed paper. Microwave for 18 to 24 minutes at MEDIUM HIGH (70%). Let stand 5 minutes.

Yields: 4 servings.

_____ · ❄ · _____

VARIATIONS

For Cornish Hen: Substitute 2 Cornish hens, cut in half lengthwise, for the chicken.

For Wild Rice Dressing: Substitute one 6-ounce package white and wild rice mix for savory stuffing. Adjust water according to package directions.

TIPS
· · · ·

For cooking chicken: Skins may be removed in advance of cooking chicken to reduce calories and fat.

Mayonnaise may be increased by 2 to 4 tablespoons for a moister dressing, if desired.

Reduced-calorie mayonnaise may be used.

POACHING OR COOKING CHICKEN
(FOR MAIN DISHES PLUS FAVORITE CHICKEN SALAD)
· · · · ·

Any recipe that calls for cooked chicken—microwave it!

· FOR COOKING CHICKEN ·

2–2½ pounds cut-up chicken	2 tablespoons white wine or sherry to tenderize (optional)
½ cup water	

· CHICKEN SALAD ·

2½ cups chicken, cooked and diced	½ cup toasted almonds
½ cup chopped celery	½ cup seedless green grape halves

· CHICKEN SALAD DRESSING ·

¾ cup mayonnaise or salad dressing	1 teaspoon honey (or sweetener)
¼ teaspoon curry powder	1 tablespoon minced parsley (optional)

1. Place chicken pieces, skin side up, in a 10-inch large flat microwave casserole or pie plate. Arrange meatiest portions to the outside and bony pieces to the center.

*2. Pour in water and wine, if desired. Cover with waxed paper. Microwave for 9 to 12 minutes at HIGH (100%).

3. Let stand 5 minutes. Remove skin and bones. Slice into bite-size pieces.

Yields: 4 to 5 servings.

──── · ❄ · ────

For Chicken Salad: Combine ingredients for the salad dressing. Toss with chicken salad ingredients and serve in a piece of cantaloupe.

· ·

*Rotate dish once while microwaving, if necessary, for even cooking.

FABULOUS DIET CHICKEN

· · · · ·

1 or 2 chicken breast halves, skinned
lemon juice

paprika
coating of choice (see below)

· ONION COATING ·

1–2 teaspoons instant onion or chicken bouillon granules

1 tablespoon dried onion flakes

· BARBECUE COATING ·

2 tablespoons plain gelatin
2 teaspoons paprika
½ teaspoon garlic salt or powder
1 teaspoon parsley

½ teaspoon onion salt or powder
½ teaspoon dry mustard
sugar substitute to equal 2 teaspoons sugar

· ORANGE COATING ·

1 teaspoon plain gelatin
½ can diet orange soda pop

¼ cup chopped onion
½ cup chopped celery
½ teaspoon garlic powder

1. Coat chicken with lemon juice and paprika. Coat or sprinkle with one of the coatings. Freeze and/or save extra coating for next time.

2. Place chicken on a paper plate or in a 1-quart casserole dish. Cover with waxed paper. (Do not cover if using barbecue coating.)

For 1 breast half: Microwave for 1 minute at HIGH (100%) and microwave again for 5 minutes at MEDIUM HIGH (70%). Let stand 3 minutes.

For 2 breast halves: Microwave for 2 minutes at HIGH (100%) and microwave again for 9 minutes at MEDIUM HIGH (70%). Let stand 3 to 5 minutes.

Yields: 1 to 2 servings (approximately 165 calories per 1 small or ½ a large breast).

——— · ❄ · ———

Compacts: For 1 breast half: Microwave for 5 to 6 minutes at HIGH (100%) total time instead of step #2. For 2 breast halves: Microwave for 8 to 10 minutes at HIGH (100%).

TIPS
· · · · ·
Cooked chicken may be substituted for the cooked turkey.

CHEESY TURKEY AND BROCCOLI

———— · · · · · ————

A great idea for leftover turkey.

10-ounce package frozen
  broccoli
2–3 cups cooked turkey,
  cubed
2 cups dry bread cubes
  or stuffing mix
1 onion, chopped
2 stalks celery, chopped
¼ cup margarine
½ teaspoon poultry
  seasoning

3 cubes chicken bouillon
  (or 3 teaspoons
  granules)
3 tablespoons flour
½ cup grated cheese
  (American or cheddar
  work well)
1½ cups milk

1. Microwave broccoli, covered with plastic wrap or lid, in a 1½-quart casserole for 5 to 6 minutes at HIGH (100%). Drain.

2. Mix turkey and bread cubes. Place on top of the broccoli. Set aside.

3. Combine onion, celery, and margarine in a 1-quart bowl. Microwave for 3½ to 4 minutes at HIGH (100%) until tender. Stir in remaining ingredients, except milk. Blend well. Add milk. Stir.

4. Microwave for 4 to 5 minutes at HIGH (100%) until mixture boils, stirring once or twice. Pour over turkey mixture. Cover.

5. Microwave for 4 to 5 minutes at HIGH (100%).

Yields: 4 servings.

———— · ❄ · ————

OVEN-ROASTED TURKEY

· · · · ·

10- to 22-pound turkey
¼ cup margarine (soft or melted) or vegetable oil

poultry seasoning
paprika or chicken Micro Shake or browning powder

Defrost turkey approximately 4 minutes per pound. For a 10-pound turkey, defrost 20 minutes. Allow turkey to stand for 15 minutes for the outside of the turkey to cool off and the inside to continue to defrost (equalization time). Continue to defrost another 20 to 25 minutes. (For even defrosting of a large item, turn the item over 3 to 4 times.) Allow turkey to stand 60 minutes.

1. Rinse and dry defrosted turkey. Stuff if desired.* Tie legs together. Brush entire bird with margarine and sprinkle liberally with poultry seasoning and paprika or Micro Shake. Place turkey breast side down on a roasting rack. Shield turkey legs and wings with aluminum foil. Cover loosely with a piece of waxed paper (or place in a plastic cooking bag that has been dusted on the inside with 1 tablespoon of flour).

2. Calculate total cooking time allowing 9 to 12 minutes per pound. Divide time in half. Microwave at HIGH (100%) 10 minutes. Reduce power to MEDIUM HIGH (70%) and microwave remainder of first half of total time.* Remove excess liquid and fat from roasting rack.

3. Turn turkey breast side up; baste. Microwave at MEDIUM HIGH for last half of total time or until probe registers 175°F. in the white meat. Let stand 15 minutes in oven or tented with foil or a kitchen towel.

Yields: 12 to 24 servings.

——— · ❇ · ———

· ·
*If turkey is stuffed, add 1 pound to the weight of the turkey when calculating total cooking time.

TIPS
· · · · ·

Always defrost the turkey, remove the giblets and neck, rinse and pat it dry (with a paper towel) before cooking it in the microwave oven.

I have cooked up to a 22-pound turkey in the microwave oven. However, a 12- to 14-pound turkey works best.

My favorite way to cook turkey is in a plastic cooking bag: Tie the legs together with string or dental floss. Brush the bird with margarine and sprinkle with seasoning and browning powder. Shield the wings and legs. Place bird in a plastic cooking bag that has been dusted with 1 tablespoon flour. Tie the bag shut with plastic tie, string, or dental floss, leaving a ½-inch opening for an air vent. Place bag containing turkey on a bacon rack or in a flat casserole dish. Proceed with step #2.

See shielding section on pages 9 and 10 for instructions on shielding.

The pop-out timer that comes with some turkeys will not work properly in a microwave oven. The turkey will be cooked before the timer pops out. It may pop out during standing time.

Compacts: Follow the same directions using a small turkey and allowing 8 minutes per pound at HIGH (100%) in steps #2 and #3.

Variation: Combination method to speed conventional oven baking: Prepare as directed above in step #1. Place in a plastic cooking bag, as directed. Microwave for 1 hour at MEDIUM HIGH (70%), turning over once. Transfer to a conventional oven (preheated to 350°F.); bake for 1 to 1½ hours at 350°F.

COMPANY CHICKEN AND RICE

· · · · ·

A one-dish meal.

1 cup uncooked rice
10¾-ounce can of chicken
  soup or cream of
  mushroom soup
¾ cup milk
1 envelope dry onion soup
  mix

2–3 pounds chicken
  breasts, legs, or thighs
Micro Shake for chicken
  or browning powder
  (optional)
paprika

1. Combine rice, cream of chicken soup, milk, and ½ package onion soup mix in a 8x12-inch microwave dish. Sprinkle chicken with Micro Shake and add to dish. Cover with plastic wrap.

2. Microwave for 5 minutes at HIGH (100%). Microwave again for 15 minutes at MEDIUM (50%).

3. Turn chicken over and rearrange so uncooked and meatier portions are toward the outside. Sprinkle chicken with remaining onion soup mix, Micro Shake, and paprika.

4. Microwave again for 15 to 20 minutes at MEDIUM HIGH (70%) or until meat is tender.

Yields: 4 servings.

· ❄ ·

PASTA, RICE, AND CASSEROLES

· · · · ·

- **Microwaved rice never scorches or sticks to the pan.** Some recipes start with uncooked rice, others specify cooked rice. Always follow the recipe.

- **To cook rice:** Combine twice as much water as rice with the rice, 1 tablespoon butter, and 1 teaspoon salt in a 2-quart bowl or casserole. Microwave covered for 5 minutes at HIGH (100%). Stir. Microwave again for 10 to 14 minutes at MEDIUM (50%) covered with plastic wrap or a lid. Let stand 5 minutes.

- **To cook macaroni or noodles:** Bring twice as much water as pasta to boiling in a 2-quart bowl by microwaving at HIGH (100%). Stir in 1 tablespoon oil, 1 teaspoon salt, and the pasta. Microwave for 3 to 4 minutes at HIGH (100%). Let stand in water 8 minutes. Drain.

- **Lasagna and other casseroles made with pasta often do NOT require precooking** of the noodles or macaroni products. Most are microwaved at HIGH (100%).

- **Remember to shield the corners of a square or rectangular pan** to prevent the corners and ends from overcooking (especially lasagna).

- If you use "No-boil" noodles, cut the cooking time of the lasagna and casseroles with pasta by one-half.

- **To cook macaroni and cheese from a box:** Mix 1½ cups HOT water with the macaroni mix (6 to 8 ounces). Cover and microwave for 6 to 8 minutes at HIGH (100%), stirring twice. Let stand 5 minutes. Stir in butter, milk, and cheese mix. Microwave 2 to 3 minutes at MEDIUM (50%).

HAMBURGER, MACARONI, AND TOMATO HOT DISH

——— · · · · · ———

Easy, easy, no need to precook the macaroni.

1 pound ground beef	1 teaspoon chili powder
1 onion, chopped	1 teaspoon seasoned salt
1 green pepper, chopped	½ cup water
16-ounce can whole tomatoes and juice	1 cup uncooked macaroni, any shape

1. Combine crumbled ground beef, onion, and pepper in a 2-quart casserole. Microwave for 5 to 7 minutes at HIGH (100%), stirring twice until hamburger is no longer pink. Drain.

2. Stir in remaining ingredients. Cover with lid or plastic wrap. Microwave for 15 to 20 minutes at HIGH (100%) until macaroni is tender, stirring 2 or 3 times. Let stand 5 minutes.

Yields: 6 to 8 servings.

——— · ❄ · ———

Variation: For hamburger rice casserole, substitute 1 cup uncooked rice for the macaroni in step #2. Microwave for 20 to 25 minutes at HIGH (100%) in step #2.

MICHELLE'S KING CORN CASSEROLE

Delicious and simple—great for a potluck!

20 ounces frozen mixed
    vegetables
16-ounce can cream style
    corn and juice
½ teaspoon seasoned salt
2 tablespoons butter or
    margarine

1 cup (4 ounces) shredded
    American processed
    cheese
¼ cup cracker crumbs
1 can (3 ounces) onion
    rings

1. Place frozen vegetables in a 2-quart casserole. Cover with casserole lid.

2. Microwave for 9 to 10 minutes at HIGH (100%). Stir in corn, salt, butter, and cheese. Sprinkle with cracker crumbs and onion rings. Cover. Microwave for 4 to 5 minutes at MEDIUM HIGH (70%) until heated through. Let stand 2 minutes.

Yields: 7 to 8 servings.

Stirring is important in most casserole or pasta dishes. Stirring brings the slower-cooking bottom and center of the foods to the outside edges. Add the toppings after stirring.

No need to precook the macaroni.

¼ cup chopped onion
1½ cups HOT water
½ teaspoon seasoned salt
2 cups uncooked macaroni
1¼ cups milk
2 tablespoons grated
  Parmesan cheese
1½ cups grated American
  processed cheese

½ teaspoon prepared
  mustard
½ teaspoon
  Worcestershire sauce
¼ cup dry bread crumbs
  mixed with 1
  tablespoon melted
  butter
paprika

1. Combine onion, water, seasoned salt, and macaroni in a 1½-quart casserole. Cover. Microwave for 4 minutes at HIGH (100%) or until mixture boils. Stir in milk, cheeses, mustard, and Worcestershire sauce. Cover.

2. Microwave again for 6 to 7 minutes at MEDIUM HIGH (70%) until cheese is melted. Stir.

3. Top with butter mixed with dry bread crumbs. Sprinkle with paprika.

4. Microwave for 1 to 2 minutes longer at MEDIUM HIGH (70%). Let stand for 2 to 3 minutes.

Yields: 4 to 6 servings.

————— · ❄ · —————

SPANISH RICE

· · · · ·

Easier than ever with spaghetti sauce.

6 slices bacon

16-ounce jar chunky style
  spaghetti sauce (or add
  1 chopped pepper,
  onion, and tomato and
  1 jar plain spaghetti
  sauce *

⅔ cup rice (long cooking)

½ cup grated American
  cheese

1. Microwave bacon between 4 paper towels on a paper plate for 4 to 5 minutes at HIGH (100%).

2. Crumble bacon and set aside. Place spaghetti sauce in a 2-quart casserole. Cover.

3. Microwave at HIGH (100%) for 3 to 4 minutes until boiling. Stir in rice.

4. Cover. Microwave for 35 minutes at MEDIUM (50%), mixing bacon into rice mixture the last 10 minutes.

5. Sprinkle with cheese. Cover. Let stand 5 minutes.

Yields: 4 to 6 servings.

· ❄ ·

TIPS
· · · · ·
Ragu Chunky Style spaghetti sauce is ideal for this recipe, or vice versa.

---

* If using plain spaghetti sauce, microwave the chopped pepper, onion, and tomato for 3 to 4 minutes at HIGH (100%) before adding them to the sauce.

EASY CHICKEN DIVAN
(CHICKEN AND RICE)

——————— · · · · · ———————

A nice meal in a dish.

2–3 chicken breasts or thighs (1 pound), skinned
1 tablespoon butter, soft
Micro Shake for chicken or browning powder
dash of paprika
¼ cup water
10-ounce package frozen broccoli

10¾-ounce can cream of mushroom or cream of chicken soup
1½ cups instant rice
2 chicken bouillon cubes dissolved in 1 cup hot water
1 tablespoon cooking wine (optional)

1. Place chicken in a 2-quart casserole, with butter and sprinkle with Micro Shake and paprika. Add ¼ cup water to the casserole dish.
2. Microwave, covered, for 2 minutes at HIGH (100%). Microwave again for 9 to 12 minutes at MEDIUM HIGH (70%). Reserve cooking juices.
3. Slice chicken and debone when it is cooled. Add to juices in casserole.
4. Add remaining ingredients. Stir and cover.
5. Microwave for 6 to 8 minutes at HIGH (100%). Let stand 5 minutes.

Yields: 4 servings.

——————— · ❄ · ———————

Compacts: Microwave for 14 to 16 minutes at HIGH (100%) in step #2 and for 8 to 10 minutes at HIGH (100%) in step #5.
Variation: Substitute 2 6-ounce cans chicken or 1 cup cooked leftover chicken for steps #1 and #2.

ONE-DISH NOODLES/SPAGHETTI

*A food the kids like to cook! No need to
precook the noodles!*

3 tablespoons minced
onion or diced onion
flakes
1 pound lean ground beef,
crumbled
1 teaspoon Italian seasonings or 1 teaspoon
oregano plus ½
teaspoon basil

32-ounce jar spaghetti
sauce (not generic)
1 teaspoon sugar (or sugar
substitute)
1 cup water
2 cups broken egg noodles
or spaghetti

TIPS

A generic brand of spa-
ghetti sauce does not work
as well as it tastes too star-
chy. I prefer to use Ragu
Natural spaghetti sauce.

1. Microwave onion and ground beef in a 3-quart casserole
for 5 to 6 minutes at HIGH (100%), covered with a paper
towel. Drain off excess fat, if necessary. Stir in remaining ingredients, except noodles.

2. Microwave, covered, for 5 minutes at HIGH (100%).
Stir in broken noodles. Cover and microwave for 12 to 15
minutes at HIGH (100%), stirring twice. Let stand, covered,
for 10 minutes.

Yields: 4 to 6 servings

EASY-LIVING LASAGNA
(LOW-CALORIE VARIATION)

———— . . . . . ————

One step, no precooking of the noodles!

1 pound ground beef
½ cup chopped onion
1 teaspoon Italian
    seasoning plus ½
    teaspoon basil
1½ teaspoons sugar (or
    sugar substitute)
32-ounce jar spaghetti
    sauce (nongeneric)

¼ cup water, white wine,
    or cream soda pop
8-ounce package lasagna
    noodles, uncooked
2 cups ricotta or drained
    cottage cheese
3 cups grated mozzarella
    cheese
½ cup grated Parmesan
    cheese

1. Microwave crumbled ground beef and onion for 4 to 5 minutes at HIGH (100%) until no longer pink. Drain off fat. Stir in seasonings and sugar. Add spaghetti sauce and water.

2. In an 8x12-inch or 9x13-inch baking dish, layer ⅓ of the sauce, ½ of the uncooked lasagna, 1 cup cottage cheese, and ½ of the mozzarella cheese. Repeat layers, ending with the sauce. Cover with plastic wrap. Shield corners and ends with 1½ inches of foil. Lay a ½ inch strip of foil along sides. Refrigerate 2 to 24 hours.

3. Microwave for 30 minutes at HIGH (100%). Sprinkle with Parmesan cheese. Let stand 15 minutes.

Yields: 6 to 8 servings.

———— · ❋ · ————

Low-calorie Variation: Substitute zucchini for the lasagna noodles—it tastes almost the same! Slice zucchini lengthwise ¼ inch thick so it resembles noodles. Omit the water. Proceed as directed above.

. . . .

Happiness is like potato salad—when you share it with others, it becomes a picnic.

CHEESE-FILLED MANICOTTI
(AN OLD FAVORITE MADE EASY)

———— · · · · · ————

No need to precook the manicotti.

· MEAT SAUCE ·

1 pound ground beef,
  crumbled

¼ cup chopped onion

32-ounce jar spaghetti
  sauce

¾ cup water

¼ cup white wine or
  cream soda pop

2 teaspoons basil

1 teaspoon sugar (or sugar
  substitute) optional

½ teaspoon salt

· FILLING ·

2 tablespoons Parmesan
  cheese

2 eggs

1½ cups shredded
  mozzarella cheese

15 ounces ricotta cheese

· PASTA ·

8-ounce package
  manicotti, uncooked

· TOPPING ·

2 tablespoons Parmesan
  cheese

½ cup shredded
  mozzarella cheese

1. Microwave ground beef and onion in a 2-quart covered casserole for 4 to 5 minutes at HIGH (100%) until no longer pink, stirring once. Drain.

2. Stir in remaining sauce ingredients. Set aside.

3. Combine filling ingredients. Stuff cheese filling into un-cooked manicotti with a small spoon or knife.

*4. Arrange manicotti in an 8x12-inch microwave-safe bak-ing dish. Cover with meat sauce. Shield corners with foil. Cover with plastic wrap. Refrigerate 2 to 24 hours. Microwave

· ·

*Rotate dish during microwaving, if necessary, for even cooking.

for 30 to 35 minutes at MEDIUM HIGH (70%); remove foil the last 10 minutes of baking time. Sprinkle with topping ingredients. Let stand 10 minutes.

Yields: 6 to 8 servings.

———— · ❄ · ————

Compacts: Follow the above directions using HIGH (100%) instead of MEDIUM HIGH (70%).

Meatless Variation: Omit ground beef in step #1. Microwave onion for 1½ to 2 minutes at HIGH (100%). Proceed as directed.

. . . .

Pleasant words are as a honeycomb—sweet to the love and health to the bones.

MINNESOTA WILD RICE
(WITH CHICKEN OR HAMBURGER CASSEROLE VARIATION)

—————— · · · · · ——————

2 stalks celery, chopped
1 onion, chopped
2 tablespoons butter
1 cup wild rice (part may
    be long-grain white or
    brown rice)

2 chicken bouillon cubes
    dissolved in 2¼ cups
    hot water
dash each salt, rosemary,
    and sage
4-ounce can mushrooms
    (optional)

1. Combine celery, onion, and butter in a 2-quart casserole. Cover. Microwave for 5 to 6 minutes at HIGH (100%), or until vegetables are tender.

*2. Stir in rice, broth, and seasonings. Microwave covered for 5 minutes at HIGH (100%). Stir. Microwave for 30 minutes at MEDIUM (50%). Stir.

3. **To serve as a side dish:** Stir in the can of mushrooms and juice and continue to microwave for 10 minutes more at MEDIUM (50%). Let stand 5 minutes.

Yields: 4 to 6 servings.

—————— · ❄ · ——————

Compacts: Follow the same directions using HIGH (100%) power where MEDIUM (50%) power is listed.

Variations: For a casserole, stir in 1 10¾-ounce can cream of mushroom soup plus ½ can of water and 1½ cups cooked chicken or 1 pound cooked ground beef or sausage. Microwave again for 10 minutes at MEDIUM (50%). Let stand 5 minutes.

TIPS
· · · · ·

I learned to love wild rice when I lived in northern Minnesota, where it is grown, and is thus readily available. However, in other parts of the country it is considered a delicacy. So, if you like, you may use any combination of white and wild rice to make 1 cup.

· ·
*Rotate casserole twice during microwaving, if necessary, for even cooking.

SOUPS, SANDWICHES, AND SAUCES

· Soups cook quickly in the microwave.

· Microwave soups made with raw vegetables or meat at HIGH (100%).

· **Reduce the liquids (used in homemade soups) by** one-fourth because very little evaporation occurs when microwaving.

· **Add salt after microwaving soups,** instead of before, to prevent vegetables and meats from toughening.

· **If using less tender cuts of meat in soups,** microwave for half the time at HIGH (100%) and half the time at MEDIUM (50%) to tenderize the meats.

· **Microwave a can of soup mixed with 1 can of liquid** in a 1-quart casserole for 5 to 6 minutes at MEDIUM HIGH (70%). Compacts use HIGH (100%).

· Always cover soups with plastic wrap or a tight-fitting lid when microwaving.

· For sandwiches: Use toasted bread for a base to prevent sogginess.

· Microwave sandwiches on **MEDIUM HIGH** (70%) to prevent overcooking.

· Heat taco shells (6) for 30 to 45 seconds at HIGH (100%).

· · · · ·

· Sauces and gravies may be microwaved at **HIGH** (100%) unless they contain sensitive ingredients like sour cream and cheese; then microwave at **MEDIUM HIGH** (70%) to prevent curdling.

· Microwaved gravies never scorch, which is a real "plus."

· **Stir gravies and sauces often.** You may leave a wooden or plastic spoon in the bowl while microwaving to make stirring easy.

· Use a 2-quart microwave-safe bowl for microwaving gravies and sauces.

· **Flour, cornstarch, or tapioca all work well as thickening agents for sauces when microwaving.**

─────── · · · · · ───────

5 large white potatoes (3 pounds), peeled and cubed	1 cup chopped celery
	2½ cups milk or half-and-half
½ onion, chopped	2 tablespoons chopped parsley for garnish
½ cup water	

1. Combine vegetables and water in a deep 2-quart casserole. Cover with plastic wrap or a glass lid. Microwave at HIGH (100%) for 12 to 15 minutes until vegetables are tender.

2. Process vegetables in a blender, food processor, or sieve until desired consistency using some of the liquid from the vegetables.

3. Return to casserole dish and add milk or half and half (for richer soup). Microwave at HIGH for 5 to 6 minutes, stirring twice during cooking time. Serve garnished with parsley.

Yields: 4 to 6 servings.

─────── · ❄ · ───────

DELICIOUS CREAM OF POTATO SOUP
OR VICHYSSOISE

— · · · · · —

2 large white potatoes,
    peeled and cut into
    ½-inch cubes
1 stalk celery (¼ cup),
    diced
8 green onions (¼ cup),
    diced
2 cups chicken broth
¼ cup butter

¼ cup cold water
¼ cup flour
¼ teaspoon pepper
1½ cups milk or half-and-
    half or light cream
2 teaspoons
    Worcestershire sauce
¼ teaspoon dry mustard
parsley for garnish

1. In a 2-quart casserole dish, combine vegetables, broth, and butter. Cover. Microwave at HIGH for 10 to 12 minutes until vegetables are tender, stirring once. Process vegetables and broth in a blender or food processor until pureed.

2. Combine water with flour, salt, and pepper, stirring until smooth. Mix remaining ingredients and flour mixture into pureed vegetables. Microwave at HIGH (100%) for 5 to 6 minutes until thick, stirring twice during cooking time.

3. Serve hot, garnished with parsley, or serve cold for Vichyssoise—as an appetizer.

Yields: 4 to 6 servings.

——— · ❄ · ———

TIPS
· · · ·

French Onion Soup improves in flavor upon reheating. You may do step #1 and refrigerate soup overnight. Reheat following step #2 before serving.

FRENCH ONION SOUP

· · · · ·

Serve as a delightful appetizer or as a meal with sandwiches.

3 tablespoons butter
2 large onions, thinly
  sliced
10½-ounce soup can water
10½-ounce can condensed
  beef broth
dash garlic powder
¼ cup white wine or
  cooking sherry

6 slices white bread,
  toasted, trimmed of
  crusts, and buttered
¼ cup grated Parmesan
  cheese
1½ cups grated Swiss or
  mozzarella cheese

1. Microwave butter and onions in a 3-quart casserole for 8 to 10 minutes at HIGH (100%) until onion is translucent. Blend in water, broth, garlic powder, and wine. Cover. Microwave for 6 to 8 minutes at HIGH (100%) until boiling.

2. Sprinkle buttered toast with Parmesan cheese. Place soup and toast in individual serving bowls. (Or use 1 large serving bowl, if preferred.) Top with grated cheese. Microwave individual bowls or large serving bowl for 3 to 4 minutes at HIGH (100%) or until cheese melts.

Yields: 6 servings.

· ❄ ·

QUICK MICROWAVE CHILI

———— · · · · · ————

Super easy; super delicious!

1½–2 pounds lean ground
   beef, crumbled
1 clove garlic, minced, or
   ¼ teaspoon garlic
   powder
1 large onion, chopped
16-ounce can stewed
   tomatoes

2 16-ounce cans kidney
   beans
½ cup water
2 tablespoons chili
   powder
1 tablespoon cumin
dash of cayenne (optional)
dash of sugar (or sugar
   substitute)

1. Combine beef, garlic, and onion in a 3-quart casserole. Cover with a paper towel. Microwave for 7 to 9 minutes at HIGH (100%) until beef is no longer pink, stirring twice. Drain.

2. Stir in remaining ingredients. Cover.

3. Microwave for 20 to 25 minutes at MEDIUM (50%) or 180°F. Stir. Or, you may simmer chili for 1 hour at DEFROST (30%). Let stand 5 minutes. Serve garnished with grated cheddar cheese.

Yields: 6 to 8 servings.

———— · ❄ · ————

To heat taco shells or chips: Microwave 6 shells or 2 cups of chips on a paper towel for 30 to 60 seconds at HIGH (100%) until warmed. Fill shells with filling or top salad with broken chips.

1–1½ pounds ground beef, crumbled
1 package taco seasoning mix
* ½ cup water or tomato juice

12–15 taco shells
2 cups grated cheddar cheese
½ head lettuce, shredded
1 tomato, chopped
1 onion, chopped

1. Microwave ground beef in a 2-quart casserole for 5 to 6 minutes at HIGH (100%). Drain.

2. Stir in taco seasoning. Add water. Microwave 5 minutes at HIGH (100%).

3. Fill hot taco shells with 2 tablespoons meat filling. Top with the remaining ingredients, as desired.

Yields: 12 to 15 tacos.

——— · ❄ · ———

Taco Salad: Stir in one 15-ounce can kidney beans, drained slightly, in step #2, and substitute 1 to 2 cups broken taco chips for shells. Instead of filling taco shells in step #3, combine 1 head shredded lettuce, chopped tomato, and chopped onion in a serving bowl. Spoon meat mixture over all. Top with cheese and warmed chips.

Mild Saucy Tacos: Use only ¾ package taco seasoning mix. Substitute tomato sauce for the water.

. . . .
*Use one half the amount of water recommended on the taco seasoning mix package for stove-top cooking.

HOT FUDGE, PRALINE, BUTTERSCOTCH, OR LEMON SAUCE

TIPS
· · · · ·
To reheat ½ cup of refrigerated sauce: Microwave for 40 to 60 seconds at HIGH (100%).

───── · · · · · ─────

· HOT FUDGE SAUCE ·

3 tablespoons butter	1 tablespoon flour
1 cup sugar	2 tablespoons light corn
¼ cup cocoa	syrup
dash of salt	⅓ cup milk
	1 teaspoon vanilla

· BUTTERSCOTCH SAUCE ·

3 tablespoons butter	3 tablespoons light corn
1 cup brown sugar	syrup
1 tablespoon flour	½ cup milk or half-and-half

· PRALINE SAUCE ·

⅔ cup butter	3 tablespoons water
⅔ cup brown sugar	

· LEMON SAUCE ·

3 tablespoons butter	1½ tablespoons lemon juice
½ cup sugar	
1 tablespoon cornstarch	½ teaspoon grated lemon
⅔ cup water	peel

1. Microwave butter for 25 to 30 seconds at HIGH (100%) or until melted.

2. Combine dry ingredients and stir into melted butter.

3. Stir in remaining liquid ingredients.

4. Microwave each sauce for 2½ to 4 minutes at HIGH (100%) or until boiling. Serve warm over ice cream, fruit cups, or cakes.

Yields: 1 cup sauce.

───── · ❄ · ─────

· · · · ·

1 pound lean ground beef	1 tablespoon parsley
1 onion (⅔ cup), diced	2 tablespoons wine or
1 clove garlic, diced, or ¼	cooking sherry or water
teaspoon garlic salt	salt and pepper to taste
2 15-ounce cans tomato	1 tablespoon brown sugar
sauce	or sugar substitute
12-ounce can tomato	1 tablespoon Italian
paste	seasoning

1. In a 2-quart microwave bowl, crumble ground beef. Add onion and garlic. Microwave for 4 to 5 minutes at HIGH (100%), covered with a paper towel, stirring once, until meat is no longer pink.

2. Stir in remaining ingredients.

3. Cover with plastic wrap. Microwave for 8 to 10 minutes at HIGH (100%) or until bubbly. Stir. Microwave again for 6 to 8 minutes at MEDIUM HIGH (70%). Let stand 5 minutes.

4. Serve with pasta.

Yields: 6 to 8 servings.

———— · ❄ · ————

Compacts: Follow the same directions using HIGH (100%) power where MEDIUM HIGH (70%) power is listed.

VEGETABLES AND FRUITS

CANNED VEGETABLES

• Microwave canned vegetables on **MEDIUM HIGH (70%)** to prevent mushing. Microwave a 15-ounce can of vegetables, drained or undrained, for 3 to 4 minutes at **MEDIUM HIGH (70%)**.

FROZEN VEGETABLES

• **DO NOT DEFROST FROZEN VEGETABLES BEFORE COOKING THEM.**

• Microwave frozen vegetables in the box or slit bag for convenience. (Place only on a paper towel.)

• Microwave a 10-ounce box for 5 to 6 minutes at HIGH (100%) or follow the package directions.

• Microwave a 16-ounce bag (pierced once with a fork) for 9 to 10 minutes at HIGH (100%) or follow the package directions.

• Standing time of 2 to 3 minutes will complete cooking.

FRESH VEGETABLES OR FRUITS

• **DO NOT ADD WATER TO FRESH VEGETABLES WHEN MICROWAVING.** Just rinse the vegetables in water, but do not shake or dry off. (This is enough water for microwaving most vegetables.)

• Microwave vegetables whole whenever possible—such as cauliflower, potatoes, squash, corn on the cob, peas in the pods (shelled after cooking). More nutrition will be retained and vegetables will be more evenly cooked.

- Pierce or prick whole vegetables such as potatoes, squash, etc., to prevent explosions.

SHORTEN OUTDOOR GRILLING TIME:

- Precook potatoes by microwaving for 2 to 2½ minutes per medium-size potato before grilling. Wrap in foil and place on a hot grill for 15 to 20 minutes.

- Precook corn on the cob by microwaving in the husk for 2 minutes per ear (remove all but two layers of husk before microwaving). Brush with butter under husks. Wrap in foil and place on a hot grill for 10 to 12 minutes.

TIPS:

- For an easy cheese sauce for any vegetable: Cover with 1 to 2 slices processed cheese during standing time.

- All vegetables should be microwaved covered with a lid or plastic wrap. (See the time recommended with each vegetable in this section.)

- **DO NOT SALT VEGETABLES BEFORE COOKING. Salt will cause dehydration.**

- Microwave 1 pound of most fresh vegetables for 7 to 10 minutes at HIGH (100%).

DRIED VEGETABLES OR FRUITS

- Dried fruits become stewed fruits by microwaving 1 cup dried fruit with ½ cup water for 3 to 5 minutes at HIGH (100%).

- To plump dried fruit (raisins, prunes, apricots, etc.): Add 2 tablespoons hot water to 1 cup dried fruit in a small microwave-safe bowl. Microwave for 40 to 60 seconds at HIGH (100%).

- To speed-soak beans or lentils: Wash and sort 1 pound dried beans. Place beans in a 4- or 5-quart casserole and add hot water to cover beans. Cover with lid or plastic wrap and microwave for 8 to 10 minutes at HIGH (100%) or until boiling. Let stand for 1 hour.

TRADITIONAL 3-BEAN CASSEROLE

· · · · ·

An easy picnic or potluck dish.

16-ounce can kidney
   beans
16-ounce can lima beans
16-ounce can butter beans
½ pound bacon
1 large onion, chopped

½ teaspoon garlic powder
1 teaspoon prepared
   mustard
⅓ cup vinegar
¾ cup brown sugar,
   packed

1. Drain beans. Set aside.
2. Cut bacon into 1-inch pieces and place in a 4-quart casserole. Microwave for 4 minutes at HIGH (100%). Add onion and microwave for 2 to 3 minutes at HIGH (100%) until bacon is fully cooked. Drain grease.
3. Add remaining ingredients including drained beans. Cover with a paper towel. Microwave for 25 to 30 minutes at MEDIUM (50%). Stir twice while cooking.
4. Let stand 5 minutes.

Yields: 10 to 12 servings.

· ❄ ·

GLAZED CARROTS WITH APPLES

————— · · · · · —————

A speedy accompaniment for any meat dish.

4 large carrots, peeled and
  sliced
1 cooking apple, peeled,
  cored, and chopped
2 tablespoons butter

2 teaspoons brown sugar
  or sugar substitute
  equivalent
2 teaspoons water
dash salt and pepper
  (optional)

1. Combine all ingredients in a 1-quart casserole. Cover loosely with plastic wrap or a lid.

2. Microwave for 5 to 6 minutes at HIGH (100%).

3. Stir. Microwave again for 3 to 4 minutes at HIGH (100%).

4. Let stand 5 minutes before serving. (This dish works especially well if made ahead and refrigerated. Microwave for 2 to 3 minutes at HIGH (100%) before serving. Carrots will be tender.)

Yields: 4 servings.

————— · ❄ · —————

Compacts: Microwave in step #3 for 5 to 6 minutes at HIGH (100%).

T I P S
· · · · ·

Do not thaw the carrots first.

One 16-ounce package frozen sliced carrots may be substituted for the 4 large carrots. The microwaving time remains the same.

T I P S
· · · · ·

For calorie watchers: You may brush the cooked cauliflower with as little as 1 teaspoon mayonnaise. Omit the mustard sauce. Sprinkle with grated cheese. (The mayonnaise helps the cheese cling to the cauliflower.)

TANGY-CHEESY CAULIFLOWER

· · · · ·

Makes a beautiful accompaniment to any meat.

1 medium to large head cauliflower
¼ cup mayonnaise, salad dressing, or yogurt (to save calories)

1 teaspoon prepared mustard
dash of salt (optional)
½ cup shredded cheese (sharp cheddar tastes great!)

1. Prepare cauliflower by removing stem end and greens. Rinse under water but do not shake to dry. Place in a microwave-safe dish. Cover or wrap loosely with plastic wrap.
2. Microwave for 8 to 9 minutes at HIGH (100%).
3. Combine mayonnaise, mustard, and salt, while cauliflower cooks, to make the mustard sauce.
4. Immediately spoon mustard sauce on top of cauliflower. Sprinkle with cheese.
5. Let stand 5 minutes until cheese melts.

Yields: 6 to 8 servings.

· ❈ ·

Compacts: Microwave for 10 to 12 minutes at HIGH (100%).

CORN ON THE COB

———————— · · · · · ————————

Once you've tried it in the microwave oven, you'll never boil it again!

1–6 ears corn on the cob

1. Cook corn right in the husk (see tip) or remove husk. Rinse and wrap ears in plastic wrap or waxed paper, leaving a small air space.

2. Microwave on a paper plate, napkin, or microwave-safe dish for 2 to 3 minutes per large ear at HIGH (100%). (You may microwave up to 6 ears at one time: 2 ears for 4 to 5 minutes; 4 ears for 7 to 8 minutes; and 6 ears for 10 to 12 minutes.) Rearrange ears and turn over halfway through cooking time.

3. Let stand 5 minutes.

Yields: 1 to 6 servings.

———————— · ❈ · ————————

Compacts: Microwave each ear for 4 to 5 minutes at HIGH (100%).

TIPS
· · · · ·

To prepare corn for cooking in the husk: Remove outer husks, leaving 2 layers of light green inner husks and silks on ear. (You may turn back inner husks and rinse corn under water, but it is not necessary. You may also brush corn with butter under husks before microwaving, if desired.)

To remove husks after microwaving: Stand ear on base and, using a hot-pad glove or paper towel, pull the husks and silks down and off the ear.

To shorten outdoor grilling time you may use your microwave to partially cook the corn. See page 216.

DELICIOUS EGGPLANT ITALIANO

1 large eggplant
16-ounce jar natural
  spaghetti sauce
1 teaspoon Italian
  seasoning or 1 teaspoon
  oregano and ½
  teaspoon basil

1 tablespoon white or
  cooking wine (optional)
½ cup shredded Romano
  or sharp cheddar
  cheese
1½ cups grated
  mozzarella or Romano
  cheese

1. Pare and slice eggplant ⅛ inch thick.
2. Mix sauce, seasonings, and wine.
3. In a 2-quart casserole, layer eggplant, sauce mixture, and shredded cheese. Repeat layers.
4. Cover loosely with plastic wrap.
5. Microwave for 15 minutes at HIGH (100%).
6. Sprinkle with grated cheese. Microwave for 1 to 2 minutes at MEDIUM HIGH (70%). Let stand for 5 minutes.

Yields: 4 servings.

Compacts: Microwave in step #5 for 17 to 18 minutes at HIGH (100%) and in step #6 for 1 minute at HIGH (100%).

Variation: Tomato sauce may be substituted for the spaghetti sauce.

CREAMED PEAS

———— · · · · · ————

If you use fresh peas, you may cook them in the pods for more even cooking. Shell when cooled.

10-ounce package frozen peas or 1½ pounds fresh peas; remove pods
4 green onions, thinly sliced

1 tablespoon flour
⅓ cup half-and-half (light cream)
dash of paprika
dash of salt and pepper

1. Combine peas and onions in a 1½-quart casserole. Microwave, covered, for 6 to 7 minutes at HIGH (100%). Drain. If peas are cooked in the pods, microwave onions separately for 1 minute at HIGH (100%).
2. Mix flour with half-and-half in a small dish. Stir into the peas.
3. Microwave, covered, for 3 to 4 minutes at MEDIUM HIGH (70%). Let stand 3 minutes. Stir in salt and pepper to taste. Sprinkle with paprika to garnish.

Yields: 3 to 4 servings.

———— · ❄ · ————

Compacts: Microwave for 6½ to 8 minutes at HIGH (100%) in step #1 and for 3 to 4 minutes at HIGH (100%) in step #3.
Variation: ½ cup sliced mushrooms or carrots may be added during the last 2 minutes of microwave time in step #1.

TIPS
· · · · ·

To make mashed potatoes: Drain 2 pounds of cooked potatoes. Add 2 tablespoons butter and ½ cup light cream to the drained potatoes. Beat with an electric mixer until fluffy. Season with salt and pepper, as desired.

To make gravy from potato water: Add poultry drippings or meat drippings to potato water to make 1 cup. Mix 1 tablespoon flour with 2 tablespoons water until smooth. Blend flour mixture into potato water and drippings. Microwave in a 1-quart microwave bowl for 2 to 4 minutes at HIGH (100%) until boiling, stirring once. You may want to use a whisk for blending and stirring to prevent lumps.

1–6 white potatoes *   1–6 red potatoes, peeled and scrubbed **

FOR BAKING

1. Scrub and pierce potatoes with a fork. Microwave on a paper plate or paper towel. (For drier skins, stand pierced potatoes on end in microwave muffin cups.)
2. Microwave for 3 to 4½ minutes at HIGH (100%) per 8-ounce potato. (Cook potatoes by weight for cooking accuracy.) Part of the potato will still feel firm to the touch. **For 2 potatoes (1 pound)** microwave for 6 to 8 minutes at HIGH (100%). **For 4 potatoes (2 pounds)** microwave for 12 to 14 minutes at HIGH (100%). **For 6 potatoes (3 pounds)** microwave for 15 to 18 minutes at HIGH (100%). (Times will vary due to size, type, and moisture content.)
3. Let stand 10 to 15 minutes wrapped in foil or covered with a dish to complete cooking.

Compacts: Microwave for 4 to 5½ minutes at HIGH (100%) per potato in step #2.

FOR BOILING

1. Place 2 pounds peeled and quartered potatoes in a 1- or 2-quart casserole. (Use a flat casserole so that the water covers the potatoes.)
2. Add ½ cup water.
3. Cover with plastic wrap or the casserole lid. Microwave as directed in step #2 under baked potatoes. If potatoes overcook easily in your microwave, microwave for half the time at HIGH (100%) and the remaining half of the time at MEDIUM (50%).

* White russets are best for baking because they remain firm.
** Reds are best for boiling and mashing.

POTATOES AND BROCCOLI AU GRATIN

T I P S
. . . . .

Betty Crocker Au Gratin
Potatoes work best.

———— · · · · · ————

*A beautiful 12-minute side dish; tastes like fresh
potatoes.*

1 small package (5.5
   ounce) au gratin potato
   mix
4-ounce can mushrooms
   and juice

1 cup water
1 cup milk
10-ounce package frozen
   chopped broccoli
chopped parsley for
   garnish (optional)

1. Microwave broccoli in the box or in a covered dish for 5 minutes at HIGH (100%).

2. In a 2-quart microwave casserole, combine au gratin potato mix, mushrooms and juice, water, and milk. Let stand while broccoli cooks. Add cooked broccoli. Stir. Cover.

3. Microwave for 12 minutes at HIGH (100%). Let stand 2 minutes.

4. Garnish with parsley if desired.

Yields: 4 servings.

———— · ❄ · ————

Compacts: Microwave for 15 minutes at HIGH (100%) in step #3.

EASY PARMESAN POTATO WEDGES

· · · · ·

A fast and tasty potato for dinner.

2 tablespoons butter
1 teaspoon lemon juice
¼ cup grated Parmesan
   cheese
dash seasoned salt
   (optional)

salt or pepper (optional)
2–4 medium-size white
   potatoes
dried parsley flakes for
   garnish (optional)

1. Microwave butter in a small dish for 20 seconds at HIGH (100%) to melt. Stir in lemon juice.

2. Mix Parmesan cheese with the seasonings.

3. Cut each potato into 4 to 6 lengthwise wedges.

4. Dip each wedge into the lemon butter and then into the cheese mixture.

5. Microwave wedges in a shallow casserole for 3 minutes per whole potato at HIGH (100%) until tender. Let stand 5 minutes. Garnish with dried parsley flakes if desired.

Yields: 2 to 4 servings.

· ❄ ·

Compacts: Microwave for 4 minutes per whole potato or until tender in step #5.

EASY ELEGANT POTATOES

———— · · · · · ————

A great potato dish for guests.

24-ounce package frozen
    hash brown potatoes
1⅓ cups sour cream
10 ¾-ounce can cream of
    chicken soup
½ onion, chopped
1½ cups grated cheddar
    cheese

1 teaspoon salt
¼ teaspoon pepper
1 cup cornflakes (or other
    cereal), crushed
2 tablespoons melted
    butter
paprika for garnish
    (optional)

1. Microwave frozen potatoes in a 2-quart covered microwave casserole for 5 minutes at HIGH (100%).
2. Stir in sour cream, soup, onion, cheese, salt, and pepper.
3. Mix cornflakes and butter. Sprinkle on top. Cover.
4. Microwave for 10 minutes at HIGH (100%). Stir. Sprinkle with paprika (for color).
5. Microwave again for 5 to 10 minutes at HIGH (100%) until done (160°F.).

Yields: 4 servings.

———— · ❄ · ————

Compacts: Microwave for 8 to 12 minutes at HIGH (100%) in step #5.

Variation: For convection microwave, Convection Microwave (Low-Mix) Bake at 350°F. (or Code #2 or Combination #2) for 30 minutes instead of steps #4 and #5. This will increase browning and crisping.

TIPS
· · · · ·

You may substitute 1 can (10¾ ounces) cream of celery soup, cream of mushroom soup, or cream of potato soup for the cream of chicken soup.

COMPANY AU GRATIN POTATOES

Tastes as if you worked all day.

½ cup milk
¼ cup butter
½ teaspoon seasoned salt
¼ teaspoon pepper
16 ounces frozen hash
  brown potatoes (loose
  pack or shredded
  works well)

3 green onions (sliced ⅛
  inch thick)
½ pound cubed or
  shredded American
  processed cheese
1 cup cornflakes crushed
  to ⅓ cup (optional)
½ teaspoon paprika for
  garnish

1. In a 2-quart casserole dish, combine milk, butter, and seasonings.

2. Microwave for 2 minutes at HIGH (100%).

3. Add potatoes, onion, and cheese. Stir. Cover loosely with plastic wrap or a lid. Microwave for 10 minutes at HIGH (100%).

4. Stir. Sprinkle with cornflakes and paprika. Microwave again, covered, for 7 to 8 minutes at HIGH (100%).

Yields: 4 to 5 servings.

Compacts: Microwave for 12 minutes at HIGH (100%) in step #3 and for 10 minutes at HIGH (100%) in step #4.

GERMAN POTATO SALAD

--- · · · · · ---

3 pounds (6–7) medium-
 size potatoes, peeled
 and sliced ¼ inch thick
½ cup plus 2 tablespoons
 water
¼ pound bacon, cut into
 ½-inch pieces
½ cup finely chopped
 onion

¼ cup cider vinegar
1 teaspoon dry mustard
2 tablespoons sugar
 (optional)
dash salt and pepper
 (optional)
1 tablespoon finely
 chopped chives

1. Place potatoes in a 2-quart casserole. Add ½ cup water and cover with plastic wrap. Microwave for 12 to 16 minutes at HIGH (100%) until tender. Drain.

2. Microwave bacon pieces and onion in a microwave dish for 3 to 4 minutes at HIGH (100%), covered with a paper towel. (Bacon should be brown.) Pour over potatoes.

3. Mix water, vinegar, mustard, sugar, and seasonings in the microwave dish. Microwave for 1 minute at HIGH (100%). Toss with potatoes and bacon.

4. If prepared ahead of time, refrigerate and then microwave for 4 to 5 minutes at HIGH (100%) to reheat.

Yields: 6 to 8 servings.

--- · · ---

A 2-pound bag of southern-style hash brown potatoes may be substituted for the fresh potatoes. Omit water in step #1 and microwave potatoes, covered, for 13 to 14 minutes at HIGH (100%). Proceed with step #2.

ACORN SQUASH WITH CRANBERRY FILLING OR BROWN SUGAR

The cranberry filling makes this a beautiful side dish for any entrée served during the holidays.

Weigh your squash when you buy it. Whole squash requires 6 to 7 minutes of cooking time per pound.

1 tablespoon brown sugar, honey, or sugar substitute

1 15-ounce can cranberry sauce

1 large (2-pound) acorn squash or 2 small acorn squash

1. Combine brown sugar and cranberry sauce in a microwave-safe bowl. Microwave for 2 minutes at HIGH (100%). Set aside.

2. Prick squash to allow steam to escape.

3. Microwave whole squash on a paper towel or napkin for 12 to 14 minutes at HIGH (100%).

4. Let stand 2 minutes.

5. Cut in half or in quarters. Remove seeds.

6. Fill with cranberry sauce and microwave again for 2 minutes at HIGH (100%).

Yields: 2 to 4 servings.

Compacts: Microwave for 14 to 16 minutes at HIGH (100%) in step #3.

Variation: For a brown sugar filling, fill each squash piece in step #6 with 1 teaspoon butter and 1 teaspoon brown sugar instead of the cranberry sauce.

EASY ZUCCHINI PARMESAN

A quick way to serve zucchini from your garden.

2 tablespoons butter or margarine	3 cups sliced zucchini rounds (¼-inch)
¼ teaspoon celery salt	3 tablespoons grated Parmesan cheese
dash salt and pepper (optional)	

1. In a 1-quart casserole dish, microwave butter for 20 to 30 seconds at HIGH (100%) until melted. Add seasonings and zucchini. Stir.
2. Cover loosely with waxed paper or lid.
3. Microwave for 4 to 5 minutes at HIGH (100%).
4. Sprinkle with Parmesan cheese.
5. Cover. Microwave for 1 minute at HIGH (100%). Let stand 2 minutes.

Yields: 3 to 4 servings.

* ❄ *

Compacts: Microwave in step #3 for 6 to 7 minutes at HIGH (100%).

EASY BAKED SWEET POTATOES OR YAMS

. . . . .

Great for the holidays!

4–6 sweet potatoes or
  yams (2 pounds)
¼ cup margarine
2 tablespoons brown
  sugar
dash of salt and pepper
  (optional)
dash cinnamon (optional)

2 tablespoons (plus) hot
  milk
⅔ cup miniature
  marshmallows
¼ cup chopped pecans or
  walnuts (optional)

1. Prick each potato or yam with a fork to allow steam to escape. Microwave potatoes on a paper plate or napkin for 12 to 15 minutes at HIGH (100%) until fork tender. Let stand, covered, for 10 minutes.

2. Peel and mash potatoes with the margarine, brown sugar, seasonings, and enough hot milk to moisten. Fold in only ⅓ cup of the marshmallows.

3. Microwave for 3 minutes at HIGH (100%) in a casserole.

4. Top with remaining ⅓ cup marshmallows and the nuts. Let stand 5 minutes or until marshmallows are melted. Serve immediately.

Yields: 6 to 8 servings.

❄

Compacts: Microwave in step #1 for 15 to 18 minutes; in step #3 for 4 minutes—all on HIGH (100%).

Variation: Substitute a 17-ounce can of yams for the sweet potatoes. Microwave only 2 minutes in step #1 to heat. Proceed with step #2.

ITALIAN ZUCCHINI SAUTÉ

————— · · · · · —————

3 tablespoons butter
3 cups sliced zucchini (⅛
   inch thick and
   unpeeled)
¼ cup sliced green onion
½ teaspoon basil
1 tomato (cut into ½-inch
   cubes)

dash of salt and pepper
   (optional)
¼ cup grated mozzarella
   cheese
¼ cup grated Parmesan
   cheese

TIPS
· · · · ·
Italian seasoning or oregano may be substituted for the basil.

1. Melt butter in a 2-quart casserole by microwaving for 20 to 30 seconds at HIGH (100%). Stir in zucchini, onion, and basil. Cover with a paper towel or napkin.

2. Microwave for 4 to 6 minutes at HIGH (100%) until crispy tender. Stir in tomato. Cover.

3. Microwave again for 1 minute at HIGH (100%).

4. Sprinkle with cheeses. Cover. Microwave again for 1 minute at HIGH (100%). Let stand for 3 minutes.

Yields: 4 servings.

————— ·  · —————

Compacts: Microwave in step #2 for 8 to 10 minutes at HIGH (100%).

To microwave squash or pumpkin seeds: Wash, pat dry, and place on a paper towel. Microwave ½ cup for 2 to 3 minutes at HIGH (100%). Salt if desired. Cool, store, and enjoy.

For crispy toasted seeds: Microwave 1 tablespoon butter in a casserole dish for 20 seconds at HIGH (100%). Stir in ½ cup seeds and microwave for 2 to 3 minutes at HIGH (100%). Cool, store, and enjoy.

Spaghetti squash is great for dieters. A 1- to 2-pound spaghetti squash cooks easily using this method. Microwave it whole. Cut when cooked, remove seeds, and twist out long strands with a fork. This is very low in calories and a tasty substitute for spaghetti.

PUMPKIN, AND WINTER AND SPAGHETTI SQUASH

· · · · ·

Or what to do with leftover jack-o'-lantern.

1 to 3-pound squash or
pumpkin (if pumpkin is
over 3 pounds, cut it
into 1-pound pieces)

Microwave pumpkin or squash whole if under 3 pounds. Just pierce rind with a sharp knife to make 3 to 4 steam outlets. (Remove seeds after cooking.)

For a 1-pound pumpkin or squash: Microwave for 6 to 7 minutes at HIGH (100%). **For a 2-pound pumpkin or squash:** Microwave for 12 to 14 minutes at HIGH (100%). **For a 3-pound pumpkin or squash:** Microwave for 16 to 19 minutes at HIGH (100%).

To microwave a large pumpkin or squash: Cut into 1-pound pieces. Remove seeds and cover with plastic wrap. (Do not discard seeds. They are great microwaved for snacks.) Whole squash or pumpkin will feel soft and yield to pressure when done.

FRESH VEGETABLE MEDLEY

— · · · · · —

1 small head cauliflower,
rinsed and cut into
flowerets
1 small bunch broccoli,
rinsed and cut into
flowerets

1 large carrot, prepared
and cut into sticks
6 medium mushrooms,
cleaned and prepared
2 tablespoons butter or
margarine

1. On a 10-inch microwave pie plate or microwave serving dish, arrange the cauliflower around the outer edge.

2. Arrange the broccoli so the stems point toward the cauliflower on the inside of the plate.

3. Place the carrot sticks between the broccoli stems.

4. Pile the mushrooms in the center.

5. Dot with the butter. Cover loosely with plastic wrap. Microwave for 8 to 10 minutes at HIGH (100%).

6. Let stand 3 minutes. Remove plastic wrap.

Yields: 6 to 8 servings.

— · ❄ · —

Compacts: Microwave for 10 to 12 minutes at HIGH (100%) in step #5.

For Parmesan vegetables: Try sprinkling vegetables with ¼ cup Parmesan cheese after dotting with butter in step #5. Proceed as directed.

For lemon-Parmesan vegetables: Increase butter to ¼ cup. Microwave in a custard cup for 30 seconds to melt. Add 2 teaspoons lemon juice, ¼ teaspoon each of garlic powder and onion powder, and 1 teaspoon basil. Drizzle over vegetables in step #5. Sprinkle with ¼ cup Parmesan cheese. Microwave as directed.

GARDEN VEGETABLE TRAY

· · · · ·

1 large zucchini (cut into 3-inch-long strips)
2 carrots (prepared and cut into 3-inch-long sticks)
2 medium-size yellow squash (sliced ¼ inch thick)
1 small cauliflower (prepared and separated into flowerets)

¼ cup melted butter
2 teaspoons lemon juice
¼ teaspoon garlic salt or powder
¼ teaspoon onion salt or powder
1 teaspoon basil
¼ cup Parmesan cheese

1. Arrange prepared vegetables on a 10- to 12-inch round microwave platter or tray, alternating zucchini strips, carrot sticks, and squash slices around the edge of the platter, and placing the flowerets in the center.

2. Combine remaining ingredients except the cheese and pour over vegetables. Sprinkle with the Parmesan cheese.

3. Cover loosely with plastic wrap. Microwave for 9 to 11 minutes at HIGH (100%). Rotate once if necessary for even cooking. Let stand 3 minutes.

Yields: 6 to 8 servings.

· ❀ ·

Compacts: Microwave in step #3 for 12 to 15 minutes at HIGH (100%).

Variation: For vegetables, use 1 bunch broccoli, ½ head cauliflower, 3 zucchini, 2 tomatoes; alternate broccoli and cauliflowerets around platter. Mound sliced zucchini in the center. Prepare sauce and cook in the same manner. Arrange tomato wedges on top and microwave for 1½ to 2 minutes before serving.

To serve cold as finger foods: Microwave for 6 minutes at HIGH (100%) and refrigerate.

CRANBERRY SAUCE

. . . . .

So easy to prepare before a holiday meal.

2 cups fresh cranberries   1 cup sugar
                                ½ cup water

1. Combine all ingredients in a 1-quart casserole. Cover loosely.
2. Microwave for 3 minutes at HIGH (100%).
3. Stir. Re-cover. Microwave again for 4 to 5 minutes at HIGH (100%) until the skins pop. Strain if desired.
4. Pour into serving container. Refrigerate.

Yields: 8 servings.

· ❄ ·

Compacts: Microwave for 6 to 7 minutes at HIGH (100%) in step #3.

DELICIOUS BAKED APPLES

. . . . .

Low in calories.

2–4 medium-size apples,   low-calorie sugar
  washed and cored   substitute (or fructose)
1 teaspoon raisins per   equal to 1 teaspoon per
  apple   apple (½ packet)
½ teaspoon cinnamon per   ½ cup apple juice or other
  apple   fruit juice
                               yogurt for garnish
                                 (optional)

1. Peel top ¼ of the skin from apples and place in a 2-quart casserole (8x8-inch).

T I P S
· · · · ·

Loosely cover cranberries with waxed paper or a loose-fitting lid in steps #1 and #3 so steam can escape to prevent boilovers.

2. Fill center of each apple with one teaspoon of raisins.

3. Combine cinnamon and sugar substitute in a small bowl. Sprinkle over raisins and top of apples. Add apple juice.

4. Cover apples with waxed paper or loose-fitting lid.

5. Microwave at HIGH (100%) for 5 to 12 minutes. (Calculate total cooking time by allowing 2 to 3 minutes per apple.) Let stand covered 3 minutes before serving. Garnish each apple with a dollop of low-fat yogurt, if desired.

Yields: 2 to 4 servings (approximately 80 calories per serving).

———— · ❄ · ————

TIPS
· · · · ·
You may substitute peanut butter chips or cherry chips for the chocolate chips.

CHOCOLATE-COVERED BANANAS

———— · · · · · ————

A food the kids like to make!

2 large bananas, firm but not green
4 popsicle sticks (wooden)
1 tablespoon margarine

½ cup chocolate chips
½ cup chopped raisins, peanuts, dried fruit, or coconut

1. Place margarine and chips in a 1-cup measure. Microwave for 1 to 1½ minutes at MEDIUM HIGH (70%). Stir until smooth.

2. Peel bananas and cut in half.

3. Insert stick in the center of each banana half.

4. Using a knife or spoon, spread melted chocolate over each banana and then roll it in chopped fruit or nuts.

5. Freeze until firm. Serve or wrap in plastic wrap and freeze for up to 1 week.

Yields: 4 servings.

———— · ❄ · ————

APPLESAUCE

———— · · · · · ————

5–6 cups peeled, cored, and sliced apples (2 pounds)
½ cup water
2 teaspoons lemon juice

⅓ cup sugar (or to taste or equivalent sugar substitute)
dash of cinnamon

1. Combine apples, water, and lemon juice in a 2-quart microwave bowl. Cover with plastic wrap.
2. Microwave for 11 to 12 minutes at HIGH (100%) or until apples are tender. Mash with a fork or puree in a food processor, if desired.
3. Stir in remaining ingredients.
4. Serve warm or chilled.

Yields: 6 one-half cup servings.

———— · ❄ · ————

STEWED PRUNES, APRICOTS, OR DRIED FRUIT

———— · · · · · ————

A whiz in the microwave.

1 cup dried prunes or apricots
½ cup hot water

sweetener (sugar, fructose, or sugar substitute) to taste (optional)

1. Mix dried fruit with water in a 1-quart casserole.
2. Microwave for 3 to 5 minutes at HIGH (100%) or until boiling.
3. Let stand 10 minutes.
4. Stir and add sweetener, if desired. Refrigerate.

Yields: 3 servings.

———— · ❄ · ————

TIPS
· · · · ·

You may add 2 to 3 tablespoons red hot cinnamon candies with the water in step #1 to produce a rosy color and cinnamon-flavored applesauce.

INDEX

HARD-TO FIND MICROWAVE AIDS

For your convenience and in answer to many requests, Micro Shake and Microwave Candy Thermometers may be ordered using the cookbook order form.

WHAT IS MICRO SHAKE BROWNING POWDER?

Micro Shake is an all-natural seasoning developed solely for microwave cooking. It includes a blend of herbs and spices that beautifully browns, tenderizes, seals in juices, and deliciously seasons meats.

Micro Shake contains *no MSG,* sugar, preservatives, or artificial color, yet boasts only 4 calories per ½ teaspoon.

A set of three shakers includes Natural, Country Fried Chicken, and Meat with Onion and Garlic.

A set of salt-free (0 sodium) shakers includes Natural, Meat, Country Fried Chicken, and Fish.

WHAT IS A MICROWAVE CANDY THERMOMETER?

A microwave candy thermometer is designed to be left in candy, soups, or casseroles while microwaving and can be easily viewed through the oven door. It registers temperatures to 325°F., which makes recipe conversion from conventional to microwave very easy. The thermometer has a paddle that can be used for stirring and an adjustable clip to hold the thermometer upright in the cooking utensil. It's a wonderful aid to candy making and can be washed in the dishwasher.

Additional copies of *Easy Livin' Microwave Cooking* may be ordered directly from the publisher by writing: Cash Sales Dept., St. Martin's Press, 175 Fifth Avenue, New York, N.Y. 10010. Please make check or money order payable to St. Martin's Press.

. . . .

Please send _____ copies of *Easy Livin' Microwave Cooking* @ $10.95 plus postage and handling charges of $1.50 for the first book and 75¢ for each additional book to:

Name: _____

Address: _____

City: _____ State: _____ Zip: _____

Total amount enclosed: $_____

───

Copies of *Easy Livin' Microwave Cooking for the Holidays,* as well as any of the products shown on the previous page, may be ordered directly from the author by writing: Karen Dwyer, P.O. Box 471, Boystown, Nebraska 68010. Please make check or money order payable to Karen Dwyer.

. . . .

_____ copies of *Easy Livin' Microwave Cooking for the Holidays* @ $8.95 $_____

_____ sets Micro Shake (3-shaker set) @ $8.95 $_____

_____ sets Salt-free Micro Shake (3-shaker set) @ $8.95 $_____

_____ Microwave Candy Thermometer(s) @ $7.95 $_____

Postage and handling charges are included in the above prices.

Total amount enclosed $_____

Send to:

Name: _____

Address: _____

City: _____ State: _____ Zip: _____

───

ABOUT THE AUTHOR

Karen Kangas Dwyer was graduated from the University of
Nebraska with a Bachelor of Science in home economics and a
Master of Arts in communication. In addition to teaching ju-
nior and senior high school home economics for eight years,
she has worked as a microwave specialist and instructor repre-
senting Sharp Microwave Ovens and as a home economist for
Litton Microwave Ovens. Mrs. Dwyer currently gives microwave presentations for television and community organizations
in addition to teaching public speaking classes at the University of Nebraska at Omaha. She is also the author of *Easy Livin'*
Microwave Cooking for the Holidays.